A Trader on
Wall Street

A Trader on Wall Street

A Short Term Traders Guide

Michael D. Coval

Writers Club Press
San Jose New York Lincoln Shanghai

A Trader on Wall Street
A Short Term Traders Guide

Writers Club Press
an imprint of iUniverse.com, Inc.

For information address:
iUniverse.com, Inc.
5220 S 16th, Ste. 200
Lincoln, NE 68512
www.iuniverse.com

ISBN: 0-595-17622-4

Printed in the United States of America

Contents

Preface

Do you have friends or family members that are making money daily or weekly in the stock market? Do you want to know how they or others do it? DO you want to know how they sleep at night while trading in this volatile market? If so, read on. What I'll share with you are some closely guarded secrets and some basic easy to understand strategies. This is a how-to book. I'll share with you the knowledge I apply to my trading profession. I will discuss how I get information, how I progress and analyze that information, and which strategies allow both a short term trader and position trader to make a comfortable living in the market.

Position trading for the individual is the stock market's hot new interest. To follow an upward or downward trend for maybe only one week and get out of the market with money in your pocket and not a care for any of the constantly changing economic scenarios is very attractive. At the end of your short trade, your money belongs to you. At the beginning of the next trade, you work in the direction the market takes you.

You don't have to ride the emotional roller coaster of monthly release data from the FOMC, the Unemployment reports or any of the other market moving stories. You don't have to worry, as you eat your dinner or tuck in your children, whether to bail out before your stock moves too much in the wrong direction, or whether to hold on to it and hope it turns the "right" direction. With the information outlined in this book you will gain the confidence to trade *ANY* stock in *ANY* market.

I'm going to use Aluminum Company of America as an example of the benefits of short term trading. The ticker symbol is AA. Let's say you know nothing about short term or position trading. You notice AA was in a nice upward trend. So, one day in September, you see the stock price increase from the opening price of $70.38 to $70.50 and purchased the stock. The stock closed at $71.00. You were feeling pretty good about your buy. **You were sure this stock was on its way up.** The next morning, however, it opened low, gapping down from the close of $71.00 to $69.63, closing even lower, at $67.88. Now you aren't feeling so good about your position. You go to bed wondering if this downward trend will continue further or whether the stock will pull through and make you money. The following day it reaches a low of $67.25. You're contemplating cutting your losses, thinking it may continue downward for a while, but hoping it doesn't. The next day it continues to reach south, so you sell it before it as it hits $66.50. You hate taking a loss on the stock. You aren't sure what to feel but you do know that what you are feeling isn't a good feeling. Then, sure enough, two days later it closes up at $72.13, and five trading days later it reaches $74.00! If only you'd held on to it…. Now, you know what to feel.

How would you like to have made money when the stock dropped from $69.63 to $67.88? When the market opened, you saw it gap down from $71.00 to $69.63. As it continued on the downward movement you sold the stock when it reached $69.50. You were banking on a one-point movement downward before you closed your position for the day and bought it back at a lower price, profiting the difference between the sell and buy prices. Once it reached $68.50 you bought the stock and made a dollar a share. You closed your position the same day you opened it, rode the trend for the day, and made money. Do you think you would have made another play a few days later when it gapped up from the close of $71.75 to $72.38? You bet you would have. This stock went all the way to $74.00 that day, but again, you went for a reasonable profit of a buck and were out. You slept well both days you traded AA. You made money the same day you purchased the stock—it didn't matter which direction it was headed, north or south, what did matter was that you were able to read and react to the stocks movement. This same scenario can be played out on a daily, weekly or monthly basis. Welcome to the world of a position trader!

My income is no longer dependent on an employer. My hours are no longer set by an employer. An employer doesn't tell me how to dress and how to act. I work for myself. My work hours are the market hours, 9:30 a.m. to 4:00 p.m. EST (although, once I achieve my daily, weekly or monthly profit goal, I will generally stop trading). I live in the Pacific Northwest, so I'm up before 6:30 a.m. to catch the market open. If I start to complain about the hour, I remind myself I could be in Hawaii. While there are many wonderful things about living in Hawaii, market hours are not one of them. The market opens in Hawaii at 3:30 a.m.

I loved trading in the stock market so much I started a business. My trading business generates an income with no rented office, no employees and no inventory. Even the tools I needed to start with were easy to come buy; a computer, some great Internet sites, a charting software, and a brokerage account. I then set up shop in my spare room.

The biggest benefit to all this is having extra time to spend with my family. My wife likes that I'm not working 65 hours away from home. My work environment is very different from a cubicle or office. The attire I wear while trading ranges from jeans to shorts to… and the walk to my office takes less than 30 seconds from any room in my house. Best of all I am my own boss. I work for myself. Topping it all off is the ability to make a great living while still enjoying life. Trading, especially short term trading has changed my life. It can change your life too.

Acknowledgements

There a quite a few people who are responsible for this book and I can in no way mention them all but I would like to thank a few. Thank you to the market makers who saw me coming and helped me part with some of my hard earned savings. Thank you to the early charting systems that all to often crashed and left me stranded in the middle of a trade. Thank you to my first ISP that would log me off just when I was ready to exit a trade and then provide me with a busy signal upon reconnection. Thank you to the Internet brokers who took their time in placing my orders and an even bigger thank you to my phone company for allowing me to connect to the Internet at a blazing 21,000 bps. Together you have made me a better trader.

Life is too short to worry about the little things. All that really matters is that a beautiful woman, my wife Catherine, loves me unconditionally. She has always been there with me and supported me in every venture I partake. It was with her help that I was able to complete this book. To you Catherine, I dedicate this book.

CHAPTER I

Know Your Responsibilities

I'm not sure where you are coming from or how much experience you have trading in the market place but I have tried to write this book for traders who are past the stage of talking themselves into being an active trader and are now serious about making money on a daily basis. I have not filled this book with inspirational quotes or motivating antidotes. What I have done is outlined from beginning to end the process of using the marketplace to create a living for you and your family. With this in mind please forgive me as I skip the normal first chapter courting ritual and jump right into the basics for the short term trader. If you are not new to position trading then you might want to jump straight to chapter 6.

TRADE WITH MONEY YOU CAN AFFORD TO LOSE. Don't trade with the money you need to pay the bills with. You've got to start with what you've got. Many of you are in a position where you will have to build up extra cash in order to make cash. Don't be fooled by wild claims of financial freedom with little or no money involved. It *does* take money to make money. The trader buying 1,000 shares of Dell at $25 has an advantage over the trader who can afford only 100 shares. If the price moves to $28, the 1,000 share owner just made $3,000. The stock price would have to move up 30 points for the same profit gain with 100 shares. For those of you with limited cash, it will take a while to get to the point where you can retire or trade profitably enough to support your family. However, on the bright side, you are making trades and learning as you go. You should be competent traders by the time you start trading in 1,000 share increments, and start seeing great returns!

Some of you are in the position of needing cash before you start your trading. It's time to get creative. How are you going to increase your trading capital? I've heard of people having garage sales, trading their cars in for a less expensive model, and I have even heard of one person selling their home to raise capital, however I would not recommend this for anyone. People can also cut back on their spending and put the money they save toward their account money. They can postpone vacation and curb entertainment costs. It isn't easy, but somewhere along the line you've got to develop some discipline for these short term trades. And if you're hurting for cash, then this might be a good place to start. Use your imagination, guided by your comfort zone, to decide how you are going to build up your trading capital and how much money you can tie up, or lose, in that account. Investing is risky business! Even if you know what you're doing, you will still have losing days.

Some companies now offer real time trading in a dummy account. You can trade in real time with a non funded account to test your trading skills. Two of the more common ones are www.Cybercorp.com a division of Schwab and All Tech, a firm based in Houston. If you are going to initially fund your account with $15,000 dollars, $30,000 on margin then trade your dummy account with $30,000 and see how you do before using the real cash. If you continue to lose money then adjust your trading style to fit your portfolio. It is easy to set up a dummy account with $100,000 and take a ¼ point daily profit on 2000 shares of a $50.00 stock. $500.00 a day or every 2 days, turns into a nice living, but if you are not going to actually have $100,000 in your account it does not matter how well you were doing. Practice trading with the capital you will truly start with. When you consistently make profits day in and day out then you will be ready for a bona fide trade.

BE PREPARED. A carpenter needs a saw, hammer, nails and an education; a doctor needs an office, a stethoscope, an X-ray machine and an education; and a position trader needs a computer, brokerage account, telephone line and an education.

Equipment. Your computer should have a modem for Internet access (the faster the modem, usually the better—get at least a 56k modem card), a CD ROM for your software (some software CDs have sound, so it will help to have a sound card and speakers. These speakers will come in handy when you need to listen to alerts as stocks hit your buy or sell targets), a hard drive and you should have a enough RAM (Random Access Memory) to run your programs. Usually the more RAM you have the better your programs will run. Most traders should be able to get by comfortably with 64 MB (Megabits) of RAM or you can double that for possible increased connection speed while using the Internet. Finally, you'll want a working port for your printer. A printer isn't necessary, but it's helpful if you want to print news or a chart on the stock. If you use, or are considering using a Macintosh computer, keep in mind not all software programs will be Macintosh compatible. You may want to research which software programs you intend to use before purchasing your computer. If you are considering a laptop computer, and the monitor or keypad is too small, then you may want to contemplate enlarging them. The larger the screen the more readable information you will be able to post to your trading screen. If the screen is to small you may not be able to see all your trading screens without constantly scrolling back and forth on your monitor. You should be able to hookup a larger or second monitor to your laptop. Windows 98 and 2000 make this an easy project. Keep in mind, if you are watching your monitor during the market hours that is at least 6 ½ hours per trading day. Some of you may be equipped to also use your television set to get Internet access. The Internet is now available to most people through their television cable company. The speed of the connection is much faster than through the average telephone line.

It is also helpful to have a second telephone line in case your Internet connection, computer or trading software crashes in the middle of a trade.

Furthermore you will need a reputable ISP (Internet Service Provider) to hook up to the Internet. There are many ways to do this, but the easiest way is to hook your modem up through your existing telephone line. After you have picked you primary ISP you might want to pick a backup ISP—I use one of the free national providers here. For those of you who can't rely on a telephone line for Internet access, you may want to consider a cable modem, DSL, ISDN or a wireless modem, such as Ricochet. Wireless modems are pricey, but you can follow the market and your stocks pretty much anytime and anywhere, depending on your reception. Cellular phones and lap top computers equip you for trading away from your home or office. A cellular phone with your broker's number on speed dial can be a blessing if you need to make that call or are disconnected from your Internet brokerage account when you want to place a trade. Also, if you only have one telephone line, you can use your cellular telephone to make phone calls while you use your telephone line to hook up to the Internet. As with the cellular telephone, a lap top computer is great to have when you need to be mobile. Unlike most personal computers, a lap top computer doesn't restrict you to trade in only one room of your home. I teach people throughout the country how to trade in the stock market. I am a mobile trader. My lap top computer and access to the Internet are essential to me. I can usually locate a telephone, pay phone or cell phone should I need to place a call.

In short, decide when and where you will be researching and trading. Determine your equipment needs. Make a list of equipment that will meet your immediate needs and list the other equipment as later possibilities. Then set up your equipment in a place to make researching and trading most convenient and comfortable for you and your family.

Two-Way Communication. You will definitely need to communicate with a broker. You need to open a brokerage account—you can't get anywhere without it. I will discuss how to select and open a brokerage account in greater detail in Chapter Five, Opening an Account. You must first determine what kind of service you expect from your broker, whether you want to place your trades over the Internet or with a live broker, and what you're comfortable paying in commissions. You can find ratings on Internet brokerage accounts at http://www.gomez.com. Narrow the list to four or five and visit each site. Some brokerage firms will e-mail you press releases on your stocks and will give you instant order confirmations of your executions. Some Internet brokerage firms give you free access to research information. Shop around and decide which brokerage account will work best for you. You can always transfer accounts if you find your broker isn't working hard enough for you or if you decide you like the services of another Internet brokerage firm. Topping my list of what to look for in an Internet brokerage firm are speed, reliability and price.

An e-mail (electronic mail) address from an ISP (Internet Service Provider), such as AT & T or Microsoft's MSN, is a handy way to gather and share trading and market information on the Internet. You can request information be sent from other web sites. They often do this via e-mail. Besides receiving market information from your broker, you may want to e-mail back and forth with a trading partner or use one of the instant messengers such as AOL's instant messenger. You can share your potential great finds, and other pertinent information, including the successes of your financially rewarding trades. When a friend of mine picked up a fast $10,000 on a 10 minute trade, you can be sure he e-mailed his trading buddies asking us how our day was. Of course, before he signed off he mentioned how his day went. However, before you set up an e-mail address, you must select an Internet browser. If you don't already have one, you may want to ask a friend or coworker which one works well for them. Explorer and Netscape are the two main browsers. As far as deciding on an ISP, I prefer a company with multiple local access numbers and the use of a 1-800 number in case I travel to a city with no access, 56K connectivity and no busy signals.

Tools. Streaming (continuously updating) real time quotes need to be live and up to the second quotes. You cannot get buy without this. You don't want to be placing trades with quotes delayed up to twenty minutes. The market could have changed directions and you wouldn't have a clue. An Internet brokerage firm should have basic real time quotes, and you may subscribe, with a monthly fee, to other real time or streaming real time information, such as news, charts, and market commentary. The difference between streaming real time quotes and real time quotes is the stream. Real time quotes give you a real time quote the moment you request it. It doesn't continually provide you additional quotes, unless you request it again, repeatedly. Streaming real time quotes show you quotes changing every second with every trade. You'll see the bid and ask as a stock is bought and sold. Your information is not stagnant. Figure 1 is an example of a streaming real time quote and chart.

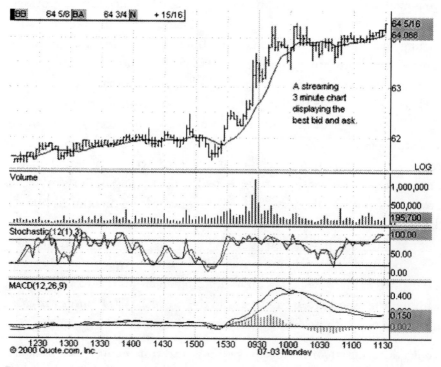

Figure 1

This chart is continually updating with each trade. There is no need to hit the Enter Key to reload the image or quote.

This streaming real time quote and chart is taken from a software program I use. It has streaming real time stock and option quotes, streaming real time charts, news with alerts, streaming real time chart scans and an extra browser to link to any Internet brokerage firm of the user's choice. You can tailor most streaming programs to fit your trading needs. A couple of the more popular ones are QCharts from quote.com and eSignal. Use the program that most closely adapts to your trading style. Look for a product with a comfortable layout and one that gives you the outcome you want. Consider the costs, convenience and the service. For example, the service may have some real time stock and option quotes, but not real time charts. Or may have all the screens you need but their data feed is slow and often crashes.

I like charts. I study the price movement and trend lines. These are known as technical indicators, which are covered in Chapter Seven. You will grow to depend on real time chart information before you purchase or sell a stock. I also use a historical chart service, TeleChart 2000, by The Worden Brothers. I purchased the TC 2000 software and opened an account to update stock charts and other stock information daily. Try using various services to help you prepare for your transaction. Some Internet brokerage firms offer a free trial period to allow you to test their advanced research features—basic charts are available on many online accounts. Decide what information you will use, and not use, with the strategies you like best. Keep in mind that *streaming real time* quotes and charts will provide you with more accurate information for you to base your buying and selling decisions on.

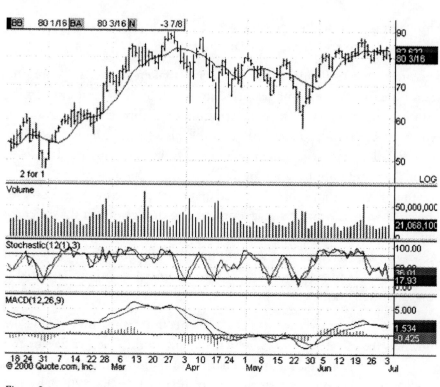

Figure 2

Using the daily chart in Figure 2, all you can see is that the stock is down for the day. It shows you no intraday entrance or exit points for a short term trader.

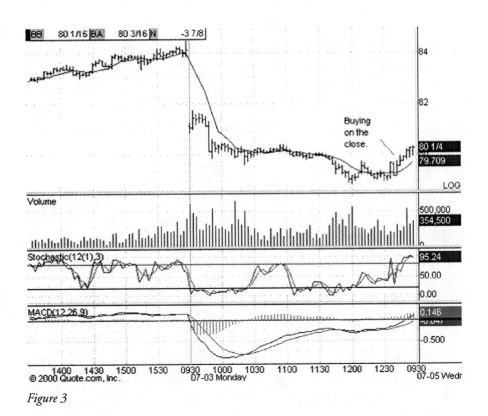

Figure 3

On a three minute chart you are able to see some buying at the close. This was a shortened holiday trading day but you are able to see around 12:30 that the volume picked up, MACD's turned positive and the stock crossed over a 10 minute moving average. During this ½ hour time frame the stock increased from $78.00 to $80.00.

The Internet features many valuable web sites offering insight, analysis and news. For access to various market-related topics, market news, real time quotes and charts, you can surf the net (Search on the Internet). A couple of free sites I like are http://www.bigcharts.com for historical charts and http://www.quote.com for live charts. Market news can be found at http://www.cnbc.com, http://www.marketwatch.com, and http://www.just-quotes.com. Most of the Internet brokerage firms also carry some sort of research. New web sites are constantly being added to the Internet. Just go browsing the web. It's easy to do, but time consuming (This is where those fast modems, extra RAM and or cable connections to the Internet come in handy). To make your Internet journey into cyberspace a little easier, I'll note, as they apply to the topic, other Internet sites. However, you should search the web yourself, as new sites are added almost daily. You never know what you'll find.

News, market news, company news, sector news, world news and more can be found on the Internet, on a pager and on cable television. Most traders I know prefer to use CNBC during market hours. A quick response from you on some great news that starts to move a stock can be very profitable. Notice I mentioned "quick" response. Excitement can move the stock price pretty fast, but it doesn't last. It is possible to be in and out of a position in less than 30 seconds. After an excited run up in the price, a stock plateaus and often heads in the other direction. The best scenario is when news is released *during* market hours so traders, can profit from it. Otherwise, the profit goes to the market makers. When Newell, NWL, announced its plan to purchase Rubbermaid, RBD, on October 21, 1998, Rubbermaid's stock price went from a close of $25.88 on the 20th to an opening of $33.00. The announcement took place minutes before the market opened. The open was delayed on RBD while the market makers figured out the worth of this news. If this occurred during market hours, and we responded quickly, we could have gotten in on the price movement of over $7 (Although, just because an announcement takes place during market hours doesn't guarantee we can profit from the news, because not all news excites traders). Not only did the market makers delay the opening with RBD, but also shortly after they opened RBD, they halted trading. Once they resumed trading again the price reached $34.25 then almost immediately headed downward. The stock closed at $32.00 that day. In this case the market makers gained most of the quick profits. Position traders depend on cashing in on news that moves stock prices, but they must be quick and know when to get in and out.

CNBC also offers market news. The news from CNBC influences investors and traders. They reach such a large audience that when a CEO from a public company is a guest on the show, a stock price often will increase as the stock is being discussed on the air. The longer a stock is hyped on CNBC, the better chance it has of going up that day. Watching and reacting to the information on CNBC is a trading strategy discussed in Chapter Eight, How to Get and Trade on News.

EQUIPMENT:	TWO-WAY COMMUNICATION:	TOOLS:
COMPUTER WITH MODEM	INTERNET SERVICE PROVIDER AND BACKUP	STREAMING REAL TIME QUOTES AND CHARTS
TELEPHONE	INTERNET BROWSER	CHARTING SERVICE
CELLULAR PHONE	E-MAIL ADDRESS INSTANT MESSENGER	MARKET INTERNET SITES
PRINTER	BROKERAGE ACCOUNT	PAGER WITH MARKET NEWS AND ANNOUNCEMENTS
		CNBC

KNOW WHAT YOU ARE GETTING YOURSELF INTO. Position trading is buying low, selling high; selling high and buying low, reacting to news, reacting to stock splits, earnings announcements, upgrades, downgrades; and starting and completing a trade in a very short period of time (1-5 days). It is this and much more. Know how you will generate money in the market with short-term plays. Whatever strategy you choose to position trade with, keep in mind the one constant, **you are in this stock or option for only a few days.** If it does not go your way get out quickly and start again. This urgency to get in and out of your position with a profit can really get your adrenaline going. Excitement, disappointment, frustration, can all be experienced throughout just one trading day. Can your personality take it? Can you lose money and get right back in there to make up the difference and profit? Do you have time to prepare research before you trade and time to monitor your position? Position trading can support a comfortable way of life, or it can be a quick way to occasionally make a few extra dollars. With a little research, and the right equipment and tools. Whatever approach you take to your trading, remember why you got in, and know the upside and downside of when you'll get out. Set your profit and loss limits, and your time limits. You are a position trader. You hold no trade long term. You will be out of your positions every few days. Your mission, should you choose to accept it, is to learn how to profit daily in the stock market. This book will not self-destruct. You can depend on it for your many reference needs. Continue now and learn how to be a *profitable* trader.

CHAPTER 2

Basic Rules for the Short Term Trader

Listening to the news and stories of short term traders, it is easy to get the wrong understanding of what a trader needs to do to make money. There can be days of extreme profit and there can be days of extreme loss. I have heard of traders making 20,000 and even 30,000 in one day. I have also seen some traders lose their life savings in a single afternoon. Along with the jubilation there is also sorrow. To maximize the jubilation and eliminate the sorrow you must not only know the rules for trading but you must accept and follow these rules. Keeping these basic and reviewing them frequently will help to keep your portfolio in the black.

BE IN AND OUT OF YOUR POSITION EVERY FEW DAYS. Even if this means taking a loss. The cardinal rule for short term traders is to only play the event. If the event is over and your trade is not profitable you do not want to hang onto the trade. You need to decide if you are a position trader or a long term investor. Both are ok, but not on the same trade. Different strategies apply to the position trader versus the investor. A position trader opens a position for a specific short term reason and is prepared to close that position within a few days, maybe even one. An investor is someone who researches a stock for its long term merits. To an investor it is ok if a stock pulls back. They are in it for the long run and can ride out the temporary decrease. The reason a position trader opens a position may be as simple as a good or bad news story or a positive indicator on a chart. While bad news can last for months, good news generally lasts only 1 to 3 days, sometimes, only 1 to 3 hours. And a positive technical indicator may last only a few seconds to a few minutes. An investor can afford a slower movement in the stock price and even hold out for some semi-serious reversals if the price decides to drop and come back, but a position trader can't. As a short term trader you must understand the reason you entered into a position, when and how you will close it and then be prepared to quickly close out your position if it goes against you. If you break the cardinal rule of a short term trader and hold onto a losing position, you are no longer playing the event strategy you entered into on your trade. The strategy you now have adopted is the Hope Strategy. I hope it does well soon. So many negative things can happen when you start adjusting your trading criteria to fit a losing play that what you are really doing is taking chances with your portfolio. What happens if a large market moving stock announces bad earning or some Economic numbers come out poorly? The market could open up against you putting you further into trouble.

PROFIT CONSISTANTLY. Profit, profit, profit. Multiple profits will ensure that cash flows in your direction. You can decide to make money from huge swings in the market with a little cash, or a small movement in the market with a lot of cash. Whatever the trade, profit. No matter how small or large, make a profit. If you close your position with a $100 profit and your commission costs are $15 to open your position and $15 to close your position, you are left with a $70 profit. Take it and leave the trade with money in your pocket. You are then ready to place another trade with your profit and look for another opportunity where you can roll into another small gainer.

Your profits should more than compensate for your losses. Profit is much better than loss, no matter how insignificant. You don't want to owe the market for your time and efforts. Also, you can record your trade as one that made you money. You want to keep score. Ten for ten is great, although not always possible. Even if you only put a couple thousand dollars in your pocket you will be ahead and feeling better about your trading. If your strategies are working, then you can up the ante and look for a larger profit.

MANAGE YOUR LOSSES. If you are losing money, sell before you lose any more of it. In addition to setting your profit limit, set a limit (known as a stop loss) as to how much money you're willing to lose if the price turns against you and heads in the wrong direction. Keep in mind; the stock price will fluctuate throughout the day, so you don't want to set your stop loss at a price the stock hits throughout the day. Set it a little lower. For example, Take Your Chances, Inc. (TYC) stock is purchased at $35 and you want it to move to $35 1/2 to make your profit. The stock has been hitting a low stock price of $34 1/2, the support line, and getting up to $35 1/2, the resistance line. The support line is a line connection of a consistently low stock price. The resistance line is a line connection of a consistently high stock price. The stock then broke the support line and continued downward. How far are you going to let it drop? $34 3/8, $34 1/8, $34? After it breaks the support line, it may hang around a lower price for a little while or a long while. You don't know. That support line could even become the new resistance line. So, set a **stop loss**. Decide how much you can afford to lose and put a limit on your losses. Set your downside limit mentally, by keeping it in mind as you watch the stock price fluctuate and sell it when it reaches the limit, or set a stop loss. If you can't watch the price, set a stop loss. You do this through your broker. Your stock will automatically be sold once it reaches the stop loss price. Get rid of the buy and hold mentality when position trading. You don't have time for it. Recognize and minimize your downside with stop losses. Then get back in there and make a profit on another trade or two, making up for the loss.

I have met many traders and of the strictly buy and hold type there seems to be a common thread that they accept and one that will be the end to a short term trader. It is the buy and hold and hope strategy. Look at the chart on BMCS, Figure 4, and you can see how it plays out.

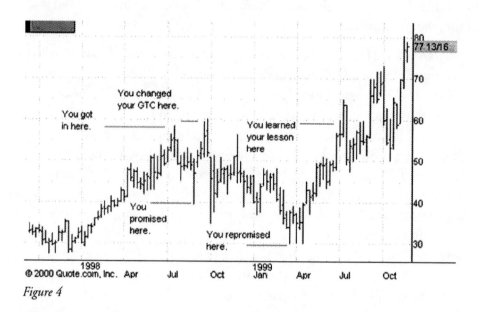

Figure 4

Paul, a friend of mine bought BMCS at $59.00 in early July. As soon as he bought it however, it started to drop. Instead of quickly selling the position at a loss he stated "This is no big deal, I'll just hold on to the stock until it comes back up." Two months later Paul still owned the stock. In early September BMCS had dropped to $40.00 per share. It had been over 2 months and BMCS was down more than 30%. Not only had Paul tied up his capital for a couple of months, leaving himself without any money to trade, he also had to live with the fact that his portfolio was dropping in value everyday. At $40.00 per share Paul made a promise to himself that if BMCS would go back up, he would be happy to break even and would place a GTC to sell at $59.00. Right after his promise BMCS started to go climb back up. One day in late September BMCS closed at 58 3/4. Starting to get a little greedy Paul changed his GTC sell order to $65.00.

"I know what I promised," said Paul, "But why not make a little profit on the stock since I've had to own it for nearly 3 month now." Instead of BMCS continuing to rise it hit $60.00 and started dropping again. For the next six months BMCS either went sideways or dropped even further. Again Paul promised to himself "I've learned my lesson, if BMCS ever reaches where I bought it I will *promise* to get out." So Paul set another GTC to sell at $59.00. Three months later BMCS closed at $58 1/2. This time however, Paul did not change his GTC and was filled the following day at $59.00. Though unlike last time BMCS did not turn back down and was at $80.00 shortly after.

This scenario is one that is played often for beginning traders. Nobody likes to take a loss and Beginning traders will do anything they can to avoid the loss, including breaking the cardinal rule—**Hold no stocks past their event!** For the entire 12 months Paul owned BMCS he was unable to trade any other stocks as his entire account was being used for the one trade. It was easy to see why BMCS hit $60.00 back in late September and headed back down. Other traders who too had bought BMCS at $59.00 were holding on until they too were able to sell and break even on the deal. Once BMCS hit $59.00 and then $60.00 there were a flood of GTC sell orders that had been sitting waiting to be filled. One of the harder lessons to learn—Manage your losses.

BECOME A BETTER TRADER. Continue to learn through reading, listening, watching, and experiencing:

Read newspapers such as the Wall Street Journal and Investors Business daily. Read investment magazines—most of these can be found at bookstores and their numbers seem to be growing each month. You should also be able to check them out at your public library. Some, such as Individual Investor give you free research access on there website if you subscribe to their publications.

Listen to others making money in the market. If they've published books, read them. If they teach, go hear them. Select books that educate you on general stock market information, and then move on to the more specialized strategies, ones that will cover your style of trading. Also, brokers sometimes teach a class to familiarize their clients with market strategies. If your broker offers a class, consider taking it. You may learn something about the stock market and your approach to making money in the market will be more compatible with your broker's. Then there are professional speakers, such as myself, who speak in most parts of the country.

Watch CNBC. Subscribe to this cable channel, and listen to what the big guys are saying. Listen; live, to what is happening in the market during market hours. You can listen to news, discussions and financial and political guests at all hours of the day. Watch the market ticker symbols during market hours. (Now in color. Red for stock prices down from the previous day's close and green for prices up from the previous day's close). Get updates on the Futures, Bonds, International Markets, and well-rounded general market news. Confused about what the Federal Reserve Chairman just announced concerning the interest rates? Listen to the analysts interpret Mr. Greenspan's message and what impact the news could have on the economy and, hence, specific sectors of the stock market. Learn the hot Index and sector for the day and why it is the one moving. Once you start trading, this will become one of your favorite channels, especially just before the market opens. The NYSE, Nasdaq, and AMEX stock market opens at 9:30 a.m. and closes at 4:00 p.m. Eastern Standard Time.

Experience trading both on paper and with real money. I learn much quicker when a lack of knowledge just cost me $500 or so of real money. Start off all new strategies on paper and when a strategy continually turns profitable that is when and only when real money should be risked on the trade. Trading should be an interactive relationship between you and your friends and or broker; there are many things you can learn from others that could possibly save you thousands of dollars from not repeating their mistakes. You may know to buy low and sell high but do you know what will happen when you put in that market order vs. limit order or when Institutional traders are most likely to move the market? Or whether you can turn around and buy stock the same day you sold it in your margin account with the proceeds from the sale? How much brokerage money are you really able to use in your margin account? Share your results with other traders. Ask what's working for them and what stocks they follow, and then paper trade your strategies before applying your real trading capital.

The best way to become a better trader is to practice. Practice perfectly on paper. Gain more knowledge and apply that knowledge to trades you make on paper (Note: You can set aside money to deposit into your trading account while you paper trade). Document your position from the start to the finish. Gather information, process and analyze that information, and decide when to get in and when to get out. Record the news and the announcements of the day, notice what impact it had on your selected stock, and record your profits and losses. Set up a system to track information, such as; the transaction date, the stock name, the ticker symbol, whether you bought or sold the stock or option, whether you opened or closed your position, the stock price, the options quote, the price at which you purchased the stock or option, the cost of the trade, limitations on the upside, your sell order price, and downside Stop Loss, your strategy, how much you lost or profited, the commission costs, margin costs, your rate of return—cash in divided by cash out, and comments or any other information you think useful to you. This may sound like a lot of work but it will make you a better trader. One common mistake made here by new traders is not following their sell orders exactly. If you cheat and say, "I would have gotten out here", it is not the same as a real trade. You must follow your stop loss and sell order exactly. Even if it means you would have taken a loss. Many traders like to say they would have made money and that they would have gotten out but did not complete the trade on paper. This is the one step that you should not skip. It is easy to get into a stock, *the hard question is knowing when to get out!*

Make money on paper. Lose money on paper. Become a better trader on paper. When you consistently win more often than you lose AND make more than you lose then do the real thing. Put your cash and knowledge to work. Pay attention because it's game time. Continue to document the news and announcements of the day, including your notes on the stock, while making actual trades. If you find you need to practice more, then practice on paper. Do sports teams continue to practice between games? You bet they do, and so should you. You'd be amazed at the things you learn both in practice and in the game, and your knowledge will increase your confidence—a definite bonus.

Continue to broaden your market knowledge and experiment and refine the strategies that work for you. Sometimes your personality fits a certain trading style, but your lifestyle fits another. Figure out what works best for you. Don't compete with others. Competition brings emotion into an already emotional profession. Know the style of trading that fits your personality and lifestyle, and compete with yourself to become a better trader.

MAINTAIN A BUSINESS DISCIPLINE. This is your business. Apply business principles to your job. Show up, be prepared, be productive, and be professional. Apply self discipline to your business. Take short term trading seriously. Granted, you can do all this in your pajamas while sitting at a table, in your favorite chair, or even on your couch, but *unless you report to work, you will not make a dime from trading.* I am up at 5:30 a.m. PST to catch the market news before the opening, and I follow the market throughout the day. I've got CNBC on in the background as I trade. I'm in front of my computer constantly checking the movement in the market and any news or research on my stock and potential stocks. I have my notes, prepared the night before; if you're up before the market, you can prepare your notes the morning of your trading day. I have a financial goal to achieve before the market closes. Once I achieve this, I can turn off the computer and get productive in other ways, until that time I'm on time and ready to trade. This is my business. I take pride in ownership, and I profit, as I never dreamed possible, from my own hard work.

MAKE A COMMITTMENT TO YOURSELF. Everything you want to do in life is possible. Commit to learning about the market and believing you can succeed. Make it your passion. Set a personal goal to apply yourself to making money in the market. This book is not the answer to all your trading questions; continue to learn. Embrace knowledge and technology. Use technology to free up your time so you can work more efficiently—it will help you succeed. In closing this chapter, I would like to share with you a Self-Confidence Formula from a book I HIGHLY recommend, *Think and Grow Rich* by Napoleon Hill.

Resolve to throw off the influences of any unfortunate environment, and to build your own life to order. Taking inventory of mental assets and liabilities, you may discover that your greatest weakness is lack of self-confidence. This handicap can be surmounted, and timidity translated into courage, through the aid of the principle of autosuggestion. The application of this principle may be made through a simple arrangement of positive thought impulses stated in writing, memorized, and repeated, until they become a part of the working equipment of the subconscious faculty of your mind.

Self-Confidence Formula.

First: I know that I have the ability to achieve the object of my definite purpose in life; therefore, *I demand* of myself persistent, continuous action toward its attainment, and I here and now promise to render such action.

Second: I realize the dominating thoughts of my mind will eventually reproduce themselves in outward, physical action, and gradually transform themselves into physical reality; therefore, I will concentrate my thoughts for thirty minutes daily, upon the task of thinking of the person I intend to become, thereby creating in my mind a clear mental picture.

Third: I know through the principle of autosuggestion, any desire that I persistently hold in my mind will eventually seek expression through some practical means of attaining the object back of it; therefore, I will devote ten minutes daily to demanding of myself the development of *self-confidence*.

Fourth: I have clearly written down a description of my *definite chief aim* in life, and I will never stop trying, until I shall have developed sufficient self-confidence for its attainment.

Fifth: I fully realize that no wealth or position can long endure, unless built upon truth and justice: therefore, I will engage in no transaction which does not benefit all whom it affects. I will succeed by attracting to myself the forces I wish to use, and the cooperation of other people. I will induce others to serve me, because of my willingness to serve others. I will eliminate hatred, envy, jealousy, selfishness, and cynicism, by developing love for all humanity, because I know that a negative attitude toward others can never bring me success. I will cause others to believe in me, because I will believe in them, and in myself. I will sign my name to this formula, commit it to full faith that it will gradually influence my thoughts and actions so that I will become a self-reliant, and successful person.

Hill, Napoleon. **Think and Grow Rich**, 1960 Ballantine Books. pp. 54 and 55.

Position trading is a new journey for many of you, and like many new endeavors, believing is essential for success. Knowledge is a large part of success. However, without the right attitude and self-confidence, knowledge benefits you very little.

CHAPTER 3

A Little Electronic Trading History

Many people believe that position trading is some new phenomenon. That it will fade as swiftly as it has entered onto the scene. What most people don't realize is that this is not something new and that it has been around for more than 100 years. Traders have been quickly booking small profits on all types of trading ever since the free market has been around. When you watch CNBC and they flash to the NYSE or CBOE trading floor you will see floor traders filling orders for their clients AND doing some position trading and even some day trading for their own accounts. It was not until recently though that we have had the opportunity that exists today. Short term position trading is constantly evolving and will continue to change as we trade more in the pre and post market and even include foreign exchanges. Fractions to decimals, bonds, futures… and the like could someday be part of the position trader's everyday regime. To fully understand what lies ahead we must see where we came from and why we are able to do what we do.

A LITTLE HISTORY
February 5, 1971. The birth of National Association of Securities Dealers Automation Quotation Systems, electronic trading. (NASDAQ). A fully electronic marketplace was opened.

May 1, 1975. The SEC busted the 183 year old tradition of price fixing on commission rates. At one time commission rates were at a set price and the same for most brokerage companies around the country, i.e. $200 for a trade with 50 shares or 500. So just to buy 100 shares of stock you needed to pay $200.00 in commissions. Then when you went to sell your 100 shares you needed to pay another $200.00, $400.00 round trip. On 100 shares your stock would have to move 4 points just to cover the commissions.

1969, the Small Order Execution System (S.O.E.S.) was started. Market maker participation became mandatory in 1988. This allows investors to buy on the offer and sell on the bid for up to 1000 shares of stock. Investors were guaranteed to be filled buy a market maker for the number of shares that he was posting, up to 1000 as long as all criteria was met (See Chapter 10 Where Does It Go?). Now the individual trader had instant fills. The S.O.E.S. was a giant step for the smaller trader.

MMID	Bid	Size	MMID	Ask	Size
DKNY	220 9/16	500	CWCO	220 11/16	100
ARCA	220 1/2	300	MONT	220 11/16	100
SELZ	220 1/2	100	BEST	220 13/16	100
ATTN	220 5/16	100	NFSC	221 1/16	100
RSSF	220 1/4	200	RSSF	221 1/4	200
MADF	219 1/2	100	AANA	221 7/16	100
DBKS	219 1/2	100	MADF	221 7/8	100
ADAM	219 1/2	100	DLJP	222 1/8	100
BEST	219 3/8	100	DBKS	222 3/8	100
PERT	219 1/4	200	DKNY	223 13/16	100
PWJC	218 3/4	100	PWJC	© 2000 Quote.com, Inc.	

Figure 5

A S.O.E.S. trader can immediately access the market maker DKNY (Dalton Kent Securities Group) and be filled on an order to sell 500 shares at a limit price of 220 9/16. See Figure 5. However if someone else SOES' DKNY first then the order would fall to only 300 shares and be filled by SELZ, (Ing, Baring, Furman, Selz). Although ARCA

(Archipelago) is next in line, ARCA is an ECN and S.O.E.S. orders are filled from market makers only.

The old pattern of calling a broker was time consuming and resource consuming. To place an order on the NYSE one calls the broker and places an order, the order then went to the trading desk, then to a clerk on the floor, then it was handed to a floor broker or possibly two, and then it was received by a specialist who filled the order. At its best, all this happened in a matter of minutes. The trader received confirmation from the initial broker after the reverse had occurred and the order had reached the initial broker *AND* the broker called you back. While waiting for the broker to call back the stock could have reversed course and any short term profits were now gone.

Today the new pattern is much more efficient. To place an order today, one only needs to hit the enter button on a computer. The order is sent to the Designated Order Turnaround System (D.O. T.) or to S.O.E.S. and then back to your computer for a confirmation all within 30 seconds.

In 1997. Smaller increments, Internet, and SuperDot.
Increments of 1/16 were allowed in all major US Exchanges. This new increment allowed for the spread between the bid and the ask to be tighter, which made it more profitable to the trader, as the market maker makes a living with profits in the spread. If a position trader bought a stock on the bid price with a quote of 43 x 43 1/16 he only needs the stock to move up 1/6 of a point in order to sell the stock at a break even price as opposed to a 1/8 or even a 1/4 point spread.

Internet access became popular and was available in most areas of the U.S. This allowed for competitive electronic trading with low commissions and rapid confirmation of trade executions.

SuperDot, Super Designated Order Turnaround, updated it rules and allowed concessions for the smaller client. Orders can be placed up to 99,999 at a time on the NYSE, and an order of up to 2,100 shares have priority over larger orders giving the small trader priority over larger Institutional traders.

With an electronic market place, Internet access, quick executions, guaranteed fills, tighter spreads and low commissions it is not hard to see why the average trader is now able to compete with professional trading firms. Throw in a personal computer, trading software and an education and you can see that we are now in the race. What differentiates the average trader from the big boys is financial backing and the depth of education these traders receive. Learn to embrace the technology that has given us this opportunity and continue to educate yourself and you will be set for the new changes in the future.

CHAPTER 4

Trading Terms

I assume many readers will know the terms I describe in this book. But it is important to understand the terminology, so I have included the basics.

THE BID AND THE ASK. The bid and ask can be restated as the sell and the buy price (although, don't restate it that way to your broker, use bid and ask). The ask is the higher price, making the bid the lower price. If a stock is trading at 32 1/4 X 32 1/2, the bid (sell price) is 32 1/4 and the ask (buy price) is 32 1/2. If you are brand new to trading you might want to remember it this way, if you want to buy the stock, of the 2 numbers posted (32 1/4 X 32 1/2) pick the price you would like to pay. It's the other one. And if you would like to sell the stock, pick the number you would like to receive. Again it's the other number. Funny, or sad, but true.

A market maker is the person who warehouses the stock for the NASDAQ Exchange. If you call your broker to ask for 100 shares of a NASDAQ stock or you want to sell a NASDAQ stock, your broker will most likely buy or sell from a market maker. Market makers have the responsibility to fill orders for their customers and the ability to trade for their own accounts. They must make a stock that they make a market in available to investors at their posted bid and ask price. Keep in mind; your broker may be looking at a screen with quotes from 30 different market makers as he is trying to fill your buy or sell order. Figure 6 is a short list of market makers along with their quote and offering size.

MMID	Bid	Size	MMID	Ask	Size
NITE	136 3/4	100	FLTT	137	300
WARR	136 5/8	100	DBKS	137 1/8	1,000
FLTT	136 3/16	100	JEFF	137 1/8	100
DBKS	136 1/8	1,000	NITE	137 1/2	300
TWPT	135 5/8	100	MDSN	137 1/2	100
MDSN	134 1/2	100	TWPT	137 5/8	100
JEFF	132 7/8	100	WARR	137 5/8	100
NEED	131 7/8	100	NEED	137 5/8	100
GBIC	130	100	GBIC	© 2000 Quote.com, Inc.	

Figure 6

A specialist is just like a market maker, a person who warehouses stock, although, a specialist has nothing to do with the NASDAQ Exchange. A specialist warehouses stock for the New York and American Exchanges. They must provide an orderly market while making shares of NYSE and AMEX available to investors at the bid and ask price. Unlike the market maker, there is only one specialist liquidating each New York and American Exchange stock. For ease of description, from now on if I only mention market maker, the term will apply to the specialist and market maker, the person warehousing and liquidating the stock unless specified otherwise.

Do you understand how the market maker or specialist makes a living? The difference between the bid and ask is the spread. The market maker or specialist collects profits from the spread, collecting the difference between the bid and ask. They sell at the higher price and buy at the lower price.

MMID	Bid	Size	MMID	Ask	Size
NITE	136 3/4	100	FLTT	137	300
WARR	136 5/8	100	DBKS	137 1/8	1,000
FLTT	136 3/16	100	JEFF	137 1/8	100
DBKS	136 1/8	1,000	NITE	137 1/2	300
TWPT	135 5/8	100	MDSN	137 1/2	100
MDSN	134 1/2	100	TWPT	137 5/8	100
JEFF	132 7/8	100	WARR	137 5/8	100
NEED	131 7/8	100	NEED	137 5/8	100
GBIC	130	100	GBIC	© 2000 Quote.com, Inc.	

Figure 7

In Figure 7, you can see that NITE (Nite Trimark) is willing to buy 100 shares at 136 3/4 and is willing to sell 300 shares at 137 1/2.

When we buy in the spread, (between the bid and ask) we are cutting into the market maker's profits. If the market maker could not match up your order that was placed in the spread your offer would be rejected and no fill would be recorded. On the other side, if your offer was accepted, then the market maker is making his money somewhere else, maybe filling a market order or filling part of a larger order and averaging out the costs. A bid and ask spread can often be found in 1/16 increments, i.e. 26 X 26 1/16. Teenies (1/16 of a point) narrowed the spread and made it a little easier for the trader to profit. When traders profit, it encourages them to continue to invest in the market, and investors are essential for market survival.

THE OPEN AND CLOSE POSITION. Although it sounds interesting, it is just as it appears. An order must be placed, to buy or sell, to open a position, and the opposite must occur to close the position. In buying stock or options, to open a position the language to your broker is, "I want to buy to open. . .." When selling that same stock or option, the language is, "I want to sell to close. . .." You do not have a market interest or position in the stock any longer when you close out your position. Conversely, you can say, "I want to sell to open..." This is used when shorting a stock (see Chapter 14) and to close out the position you would say "I want to buy to close..."If you use an Internet broker, then you open your position with a stock or option and you close it by placing your order and selecting the stock or option already in your portfolio. This language helps keeps your trades in order. Without it, you may have several positions open on a stock.

For example, if you purchased 100 shares of American Online (AOL) and you wanted to sell the stock to close your position, you need to sell to close 100 shares from your portfolio. If you don't indicate you want to sell to close, or work with the stock you currently have in your portfolio, then you may start, or open, another transaction. Sometimes this can be a little tricky if you have a stock and an option interest in one stock. For example, you open your position when you make your first transaction on a stock. You **buy the stock** in AOL and **sell an option** on AOL. Both of these orders are open positions, even though you have a buy and sell. The close position completes the transaction; it does not start another one. These positions will be closed when you **sell the stock** in AOL and you **buy the option** in AOL.

DAY ORDER VS. GTC. When placing your trade, you will need to specify the duration of your order. You specify whether you want either a day order or a GTC order. A day order is just as it appears. The order is only good for the day. If your order is not executed the day you place it, then it will expire at the end of the trading day. Be sure to confirm with your broker just what time their trading day ends, as many are now open for after hours trading. You will not be charged for your order unless it is filled. There is no need to cancel your order after the close of the market day, it just disappears. However, Good Till Canceled (GTC) is something completely different. A GTC is an order that lasts until it is canceled or it expires, generally 60 to 90 days depending on your brokerage firm. You will rarely use a GTC to open a new position in position trading. Why? Well, if you enter into a position trade you are generally just trying to trade a specific event. Whether it is a news event or a technical event, you are only trying to capture a small move in the stock. You do not have the luxury of placing an order and forgetting about it. Your trade may be completed in as little as 1–5 days. You will need to monitor your trade for the exact time needed to maximize your profit. If you do use a GTC it will most often be used on the sell side of your order. If you purchased a stock or option and plan to sell when the stock hits a short term resistance then you may wish to consider a GTC to sell just slightly beneath the resistance. Before you spend any of your hard-earned cash, know what you are doing and why, from the open position to the close position. A GTC is great for a position trade, but only on the sell side of the order.

LIMIT ORDER VS. MARKET ORDER. A limit order states you will buy or sell the stock or option at a specific, limited, price. If you place an order to buy shares at a limit of $26, your order will not be executed at $26 1/16. You will only be filled at $26 or better, so you could even be filled at $25 27/32. A little trick when placing your order to buy or sell is to not place an even amount order, such as 26. Although some orders are filled at 26, even more are filled at a price slightly above or below the even amount price. The market maker can see all the orders to buy and sell and knows how many orders are waiting to be sold at 26. The market maker may raise the price to just below $26. As you get more and more frustrated because you are not able to sell your stock and move on, you lower your price well below $26 and take less of a profit. Guess who gets the profit you left behind? Place your order just above an even amount price, if you want to buy on a dip, or just below if you're in a hurry to sell on the way down. Think about every time you buy a stock what number do you place to sell it at. If you bought a stock at 26 1/4 would you be happy to sell it for 27.00 on the same day? So would others and this is why you will find resistance at whole numbers. When was the last time you placed an order to sell at 26 15/16? Lots of open room for you to get filled as everyone else has their order placed to sell at 27.00. Here you can see the whole number theory at work. Look at all the support at 45.00 in Figure 8

MMID	Bid	Size	MMID	Ask	Size
MLCO	45	1,000	MONT	45 3/16	100
AANA	45	1,000	SELZ	45 3/16	100
GRUN	45	900	RSSF	45 5/16	100
RSSF	45	100	LEGG	45 3/8	300
LEHM	45	100	COWN	45 3/8	100
PERT	45	100	JPMS	45 7/16	1,000
RAJA	45	100	AANA	45 9/16	1,000
JANY	45	100	MLCO	45 11/16	1,000
HAMR	45	100	PERT	© 2000 Quote.com, Inc.	

Figure 8

The other choice is to use a market order. When filling a market order your trade can be filled at a price more convenient to the market maker than to you. This is known as slippage and happens when the market maker fills your order at 1/4 to a 1/2 point or so in their favor. This could really hurt your trading profit if there is any left after being filled with a market order. *A market order can be the kiss of death.* You lose control of your planned open and close position. You get strung along by the market maker's choice. Who do you think cares more about your profits, the market maker or you? Let's say a stock price starts to move upward on some really good news. It's moved three points in the last half hour. You place a market order to buy the stock. You get the stock all right, but sometimes at a 1/2 point or so higher than the quote you received when you placed the order. The market maker was so busy filling the limit orders that when he finally got to yours, the price was much higher. Then you found out you bought the stock on the high of the day and it headed downward. Where is your profit now? What do you do? Exit immediately? You have to come up with a new plan, and albeit it will be an emotional one at that. The market maker wants your money, and a market order hands it over. Now, there are times, very few, when a market order is okay, but not for position trading. Know the limit price of what you will pay for a stock or option and the limit price of where you will sell it. Say you want to buy 500 shares of Disney stock. It is trading at 26 X 26 1/4. The language you would use to place the order is, "I want to **buy 500 shares of Disney, ticker DIS, at a limit of 26 1/4 for the day.**" Don't flirt with death; eliminate the market order from your position trading vocabulary.

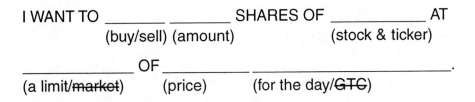

I WANT TO _____ _____ SHARES OF _____ AT
       (buy/sell) (amount)   (stock & ticker)

_____ OF _____ _____.
(a limit/~~market~~)   (price)   (for the day/~~GTC~~)

SHORT SELLING. Short selling, in most cases, can only be done on an up tick. An up tick is an increase in the price of the stock where the ask price has increased in value. Most of us were taught the one golden rule for making money in the market. Buy low and sell high. No one ever told us that it could also be done backwards. Sell high and *then* buy low. You sell the stock at its high, wait for it to drop back to its low, buy it, and you keep the difference, minus commissions. In Figure 9 you can see the stock dropping below its 10 minute moving average while the Stochastics and MACD's are both showing a sell signal.

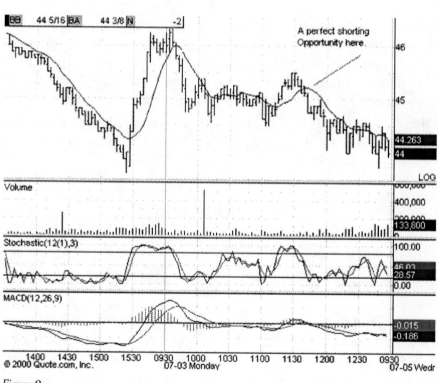

A perfect shorting
Opportunity here.

Figure 9

When Chris, a trading partner of mine, tried shorting for his first time, he profited $1,375 before paying commissions. Just one week after taking my Short Term Trading Seminar, he had the confidence to do a short sell play. On October 7, 1998, Chris and a friend of his were watching Compaq Computer, (CPQ). His friend bought CPQ at 27 1/2 (thinking he was getting the stock at a low as it was dropping in price), but Chris thought the price would continue to drop. So, he SOLD 1,000 shares of CPQ at 26 11/16, and later that day BOUGHT it at a lower price of 26 5/16, pocketing the difference (If you sell it for more than you paid for it, then you profit). Chris made $935 on that play, so he tried it again that same day on the same stock. He sold to open his position at 25 13/16 and bought to close his position at 25 1/4, making an additional $440.

1) This play can only be done in a margin/short account.
2) The language used to place this trade would be, "I would like to sell short 500 shares of CPQ at a limit of 25 13/16 for the day." The downside to this strategy, of course, is if the stock price goes up and you have to buy it at a higher price. Ouch!
3) Unless shorting as a market maker, a short sell can only be done on an up tick.

Short Squeeze. When shorting a stock you need to pay special attention to upcoming news events that might spark a buying rally. These events might include an earnings announcement, a stock split, a favorable economic number, upgrades, or new product orders. If there is heavy short selling on a stock any positive news could send traders scrambling to cover their positions. Combine the positive news on a stock with thousands of traders buying to cover their position before the stock climbs too high and you can see what might happen. This is called a short squeeze. When shorters are squeezed out of their positions in a hurry, you can have some huge price run ups in a very short time period. To see the amount of short interest on a stock visit www.viwes.com. This site will clue you in on how many shares of a Nasdaq stock have been sold short and have not yet been bought back to cover. Any positive news on the heavily shorted stocks on this list could have an extremely positive effect on the stocks price.

CASH VS. MARGIN ACCOUNT. A position trader is anyone that completes a trading transaction, opens and closes a position, in 1 day or up to 1 month. To be more specific, you are just trying to profit from a small move in the stock. Sometimes it will be possible for you to enter into and even exit a trade on the same day. When this type of transaction is conducted in a *cash* account involving *stock* transactions, the *T + 3 Rule* applies. The T + 3 Rule states the money needed to purchase a security must be in your account by the third day following the trading day. "T" is the trading day. "3" is 3 additional business days. So, if an order was placed on Monday (Monday = T, Tuesday = day 1, Wednesday = day 2, and Thursday = day 3), by Thursday afternoon all the money needed to complete the transaction must be in your account. The T + 3 Rule also applies when you sell your stock. The profits from the sell of a transaction cannot be used until three days after the trading date. In the above example, you could buy and sell stock with that money on Thursday. If you try to reuse the money before the third day following the trading day, a restriction may be placed on your account enforcing the SEC regulation. If you are unable to come up with additional funds to pay for your trade your account will acquire an SEC violation. This is called a Regulation T violation. If you receive a Regulation T violation in your account, you will not be allowed to withdraw any funds from your account for the next 90 days. If this happens 3 times within a 12 month period your account will be closed. The SEC takes this rule seriously.

A cash account is necessary for option trading, but the T + 1 Rule applies to options. When a transaction is conducted in a *cash* account involving *option* transactions, then the *T + 1* Rule applies. Money from an option trade in a cash account can be used the following day after closing your position trade. So, if you're trading options in your cash account, the T + 1 Rule is the rule. If you buy an option on Monday and sell it on Monday, you can reuse the money for another trade on Tuesday. Both the T + 1 and T + 3 are for your cash accounts. If you are a day trader you will want to use your margin account where neither the T + 1 or T + 3 Rule applies.

A margin account helps your money go twice as far. It can only be used to purchase and sell stocks. Options cannot be purchased in your margin account. The SEC rates options trading as a risky venture and will not let a trader trade with borrowed margin money on options. You will need at least $2,000 to open your margin account—read your Margin Account Agreement for the specific details. If a stock is purchased on margin, the broker can lend you up to 50% of the total purchase price. If you open a margin account with $5,000, your broker can match that amount and you now have $10,000 of buying power. If you use margin money, you will be charged, on average, an interest rate of approximately 8% per year on the money. You will only be charged margin interest if you use the margin money in your account. When you buy stock in your margin account your initial $5,000 is used first, when you use the remaining $5,000 you will then be charged interest while you are using the brokers money. That means you can buy Yahoo (YHOO) at half the stock price on margin, minus a small margin interest cost and commission. A T + 1 minus Rule applies to margin accounts. Same day trading (Day trading) in your margin account tops the cash T + 1 Rule. There are no T + Rules *If* you buy and sell, open and close your position, the same day in your margin account. If you buy a stock and then sell the stock on the same day, you can reuse the money again the same day. You can do this as many times as you can before the market closes. And you pay no margin interest costs, as long as you don't hold your position overnight! You can buy and sell YHOO on Thursday, and with the same money buy and sell more YHOO stock several times that same day. In some brokerage firms such as National Discount Brokers you may also only be charged commission on the first buy and sell order as long as it is the same stock on the same day. So if you bought YHOO in your margin account on Monday and sold it on Monday you would pay commissions for the trade but then could reuse the money in your margin account for another trade the same day. If you chose to buy and sell YHOO again you would not be charged any more commissions for the second order. Margin interest rates apply to stock held overnight. You will only be charged a fee if you hold a position of margined money overnight. So, if you buy a stock on Monday and hold it overnight to sell on Tuesday, you will pay a margin interest rate and to top it off since you did hold the stock overnight the T + 1 Rule now applies. If you sell your stock on Tuesday that you bought on Monday you will not be able to reuse the cash until Wednesday. An example would be if you purchased 1000 shares of CPQ on Monday for 26 and sold it on Tuesday for 26 1/2, you would not be able to use *ANY* of the funds you received from the sale of CPQ until Wednesday. You would however, be able to reuse the 26,000 on Monday if you sold it the same day you purchased it on.

CHAPTER 5

Open an Account

When you select a brokerage firm, you are deciding you want a relationship with that firm. You are satisfied with the commission fees; the research or advice available; their reputation for reliability as far as speed and accuracy of executing your transaction; their availability—they are or an assistant is always available in a reasonable amount of time; the information you receive is always available to you during market hours (sometimes with Internet accounts all or part of the system may not be available); and other criteria as the list goes on.

Your first step in choosing a broker is to decide whether you prefer to use a full service, discount, or Internet brokerage firm. You need to decide which is right for you. If you choose a full service broker, then you will want to make sure you are never put on hold, are quickly filled on your orders and are receiving a reduced commission rate (since you are doing all your own research and only need an order taker). The last thing you need, as a short term trader, is to exit a trade in a hurry and sit on hold as you watch your stock drop and profits erode. Also, your broker should always be available before the market opens, during market hours and after the market closes. If this is the case, then you've got a broker dedicated to availability in servicing clients. Availability is an excellent quality to find in a broker. Another good quality is flexibility—flexibility with commission costs. If you're placing 1 to 10 round trip trades a week with your broker, and you're doing the research, then you should be able to negotiate a reduced commission fee. I choose not to use a full service broker, for position trading, because I don't want to pay for services I don't use. Consider using a discount broker if availability and reduced commission costs are not offered at your brokerage firm.

Another choice, and the one I prefer for short term position trading, is an online broker. Since I'm online using a real time charting service, it only makes since to place my trades online. Most online brokers offer the same services that a live broker offers, but with added benefits like commissions from $10.00 for limit orders up to 1000 shares and instant order executions and conformations. They allow you to buy long, sell short, trade options and even place your trades 24 hours a day. Perhaps you want a full service broker with Internet availability or you may want multiple accounts—a discount service broker and an Internet account. And there are many of you who want nothing to do with a service broker, be it full, discount or even deep discount. You trade only electronically. However, even with an Internet account you want access to trade over the telephone in the tragic event your PC crashes, your trading site is down or you're not at your computer. In any event, it is probably in your best interest to have a couple, if not several accounts. It doesn't hurt to be prepared for the unexpected. I've even heard of people getting a second phone line by another telephone carrier in case one line goes down. It's all up to you. Let me show you how two accounts can aid in the event one account experience some problems. In account 1 you buy 1000 shares of CIEN at $26.00. When CIEN reaches $28.00 you place your order to sell, but as you do, your online broker experiences some problems. You don't want to lose your profits, so you go to account 2. In account 2 you sell short 1000 shares of CIEN at $28.00. If CIEN goes up you will lose profits in account 2 but make the exact amount back in account 1. If CIEN goes down you will make a profit in account 2 but lose the exact amount in account 1 locking in your initial profit of $2.00.

ACCOUNT 1

1) Plan:
   Buy 1000 shares of CIEN @ $26
   Sell 1000 shares of CIEN @ $28

2) Action:
   Bought 1000 shares of CIEN
   @ $26(Access to Internet account
   cut off. Can't sell at @ $28)

5) Internet Account is working again
   Stock is @ $27

6) **Sold** 1000 shares of CIEN @ $27
   YOU MAKE A $1 PROFIT!

ACCOUNT 2

3) Plan:
   Sell 1000 shares of CIEN @ $28
   Buy 1000 shares at sell price in
   Account 1

4) Action:
   Sold 1000 shares of CIEN
   @ $28

7) Action:
   Bought 1000 shares of
   CIEN @ $27
   YOU MAKE A $1 PROFIT!

Total profit on the trade is $1 in each account, totaling $2, minus commissions. Initial plan was to make $2 on the play. These situations don't happen often but a backup is always good business. Your ability to profit in your second account when access to the first account is cut off will also improve your mental outlook. If you really want to get your blood boiling all you need to do is watch your profit erode tick by tick by tick as you place an order on your computer only to find out that there servers are busy and your order status reads "Pending" for the next ten minutes.

As a basic rule I will not use a full service broker for position trading. Full service brokers are as their name implies, a full service broker. Because they are a full service broker their business is really set up for the investor and not for the trader. What I want are quick accurate fills, reliability and a low commission. Today these four items can be found in abundance from Internet brokers. Check out www.cyberinvest.com for a listing of both electronic and web based brokers and the differences between each. If you are not comfortable doing your own research because you don't have the tools or trust your knowledge base yet, then you should wait to position trade until you are ready. After studying this book and applying the techniques I have prepared and outlined, you will have the tools and the confidence you need to generate a consistent cash flow into your account.

Before selecting an Internet brokerage firm, you may want to shop around. Another web site that rates Internet brokerage firms is www.gomez.com. This service is provided by Gomez Advisors, Inc. It is by no means a complete list of every Internet broker but it is an excellent place to begin. At the time of this writing they rated over 50 Internet brokerage firms. This site not only lists brokerage firms, but it rates their various services from 1 to 10. They rate the firms by category and profile. If you select to see the ratings by category, you can choose to see the top firms on their list rated by 1) overall score; 2) ease of use; 3) customer confidence; 4) on-site resources; 5) relationship services, and 6) overall cost. If you choose to see the ratings by profile, you can view their highest ratings for 1) hyper-active trader; 2) serious investor; 3) life goal planner, and 4) one-stop shopper. For some traders with little computer experience, the "ease of use" category may be very important for them to review. For others, overall cost may be the top requirement when they select a brokerage firm. For position traders, check the hyper-active trader profile.

For many short term traders a basic dial up Internet account should meet their needs. Position traders using active charting screens and real time stock screening may want to consider a high speed DSL or cable line to the marketplace. You can find these services, as well as other Internet brokerage firms, by browsing the web. When I searched the web under "Stock Quotes" and "Internet Trading" I pulled up another list of Internet accounts (the search words may vary depending on your browser, but you get the idea). Some brokerage firms on this list were also on the Gomez list, but many were not. The search also pulled up firms trading with NASDAQ Level II data. The firms using Level II data may require anywhere from $15,000.00 to $60,000.00 to open a margin account. One firm offering Level II data also offered free, the standard Level I data with an opening margin requirement of $3,000.00.

As you may know, I am not a broker and cannot recommend investments or give advise on your portfolio. This forces you to think for yourself, to do your own research. I share with you what I do and let you know where information and brokers are located. It's up to you to decide how to use the information. I didn't say this would be easy. There are so many different routes to take. Take the route that best fits your needs and personality. If you find you don't like the services of one brokerage firm, you can always transfer your account to another firm. Here's a little treat for your shopping; when checking out a brokerage web site, make sure to check out the resources or research section. Whether you decide to use the firm or not, you may learn of additional web sites to add to your Favorites list. You may find you really like a certain brokerage firm, but don't need their expensive services yet. Someday, if you need more from your broker, you'll know where to check.

The benefits of trading on the Internet are cost and efficiency. Trades may range from $5.00 to $30.00 for commission fees on equity (stock) transactions. Commission fees for options are typically higher than you'd pay for equities but still usually less than those from a live broker. Confirmation of your transaction should be quick, three seconds for some and no more than 60 seconds for others. You will usually receive confirmation of your transaction within a few seconds, depending on your service. When shopping, for an online trading account, ask for the average order confirmation time. Five minutes is not a quick response time. It should be under 60 seconds, 3 seconds is better, depending on the volume of the stock traded. Many Internet firms provide great research data and links to resourceful market information. The Internet places information, once only available to brokers, at the fingertips of the individual investor. Once you get a hold of this information and see how the technical indicators correlate to the stock price, you'll wonder how you ever got along without it. If you place a trade with a broker, you may feel like you are putting your trust in a broker and working blindly, but that is what most investors do—they may look at old information and rely on their broker for current information. What most investors do not realize is that their broker may or may not know how to be a successful position trader.

When you enter into a short term position trade, speed and timing of your executions are the main considerations. Long term buy and hold investors may not understand this concept. They may think of nothing more than to hold on to the security and wait for it to head the "right" direction. Keep in mind; most brokers specialize in investing, rather than trading. After reading this book, if you use a broker, you may want to share with him or her your goals and expectations on position trading. They'll get it, although some might try to steer you towards investing and not trading. You may become a squeaky wheel, needing information and or assistance daily. They'll have to pay attention to you. If you're bent on position trading and using a service broker, try looking for a broker who specializes in the type of trading you want to do. They'll be expecting to hear from you.

Whatever brokerage firm you use, make sure it's cost effective and responsive to your needs. Once you've done the hard part and selected a brokerage firm, all the paperwork (the Customer Agreement including each markets agreement may be 30 pages long) needs to be completed and decisions as to what types of accounts to open need to be made. Which accounts do you open? Cash, margin, short, options or all of the above? And of course, each account has its own paperwork. You might want to check off each box for types of accounts. Even if you have no intention of trading options or selling short at this time, you may in the future. You don't want to run into a situation where you have what you believe to be an ideal buying situation only to find out that you have not been approved to enter the transaction because you did not fill out the necessary paperwork.

As in most forms of business, leverage is an important tool. In the stock market leverage comes in the form of margin. Margin can be your best friend when you are making money and a burden to your existence when you are losing money. Here is how it works. You open up your brokerage account and put in $5000.00. Your brokerage house matches you up to a certain price point and also puts in $5000.00 so that you now have $10,000.00 worth buying power. The amount that your brokerage house will lend you is determined buy your past experience in the stock market and your cash assets. This amount could be as high $100,000.00 or more but in most cases will never exceed the amount that you deposited into your account. So if you deposit $25,000.00 into your account your broker will match that amount giving you $50,000.00 of buying power. Although this may seem to be an unsecured loan your brokerage firm will hold the stock you purchased as collateral for the loan. You might ask why a brokerage house would lend you money to buy stocks. The answer is really quite simple. Fees! You will be charged margin fees to use the money and in many cases traditional investors are generally charged more commission fees for larger orders. Here is the neat part for short term traders; if you buy a stock today and sell the same stock today you are not charged any margin fees. You are only charged margin fees if you hold the stock overnight. Another great reason for trading in your margin account has to do with the frequency of trades. In a cash account, if you buy a stock today and sell it today you are not allowed to reuse the money involved in the trade for 3 more business days. It is referred to as the T+3 rule or trade plus 3. So in our original scenario with a brokerage account that contains $10,000.00 worth of buying power, you purchase $10,000.00 worth of stock in your cash account on Monday and sell it on Tuesday. You will not be able to reuse the money again until Friday, T+3. However, in your margin account, if you buy the stock on Monday and sell it on Tuesday you can reuse it again on Wednesday. In your margin account the rule is T+1. Now for the really good part. If you purchase stock on Monday and sell it on Monday, you can reuse it again on Monday over and over and over… giving you unlimited buying potential.

Now before you start equating margin with a cure for cancer or an inexpensive eternal non polluting fuel source let me fill you in on the dark side. First off and most important is that when you lose money you are really losing twice as much since half of what you lost was borrowed money. The quickest way to drain your account is to lose on margin. Second, not all stocks are marginable although most stocks that are above $5.00 are marginable. You might find out that a stock is marginable with Merrill Lynch but not with Schwab. It is up to each brokerage house to decide if a stock is marginable since they are the ones lending you the money to purchase the stock. Third, you could at some point in time get a phone call from your broker throwing you into a state of panic by saying 5 little words. "You have a margin call." A margin call is a call from your broker asking you to deposit additional funds into your account. If your broker loaned you $5,000.00 to purchase stock and the value of the stock is currently only worth $4,000.00 you will receive a $1,000.00 margin call giving you 3 days to deposit the additional funds or sell stock to cover your shortfall. If you fail to deposit funds in the time allowed your broker will sell stock from your account to cover. Fourth and not to be overlooked is a Fed Call or otherwise known as a regulation T violation. It is similar to a margin call but you cannot sell stock from your account to cover. You must send in cash to cover the call. If you do not send in the cash your account will be placed on restriction for 90 calendar days. Although you will be able to access your account and trade, you will not be allowed to withdraw any funds. If you receive multiple Fed Call violations you stand the chance of having your account closed. To receive a Fed Call all you need to do is purchase stock and sell it and then not wait the specified time before reusing the money again. For example, in your cash account instead of waiting T+3 you reuse the money from a trade you reuse it at T+2. Or in your margin account if you purchase a stock on Monday and sell it on Tuesday you must wait until Wednesday to reuse the money again, T+1. If you don't wait until Wednesday and purchase more stock on Tuesday with the money from Mondays purchase you will create a Fed Call for yourself. Fifth, options are not marginable, only stocks.

If you want the ability to short the stock, to sell the stock when you don't own it, then you've got to complete another form for a Short Account. This account usually requires a higher balance in it before getting approval to trade the stock short, because it's riskier than selling the stock when you own it. If you want to only play stocks, and not the options, you may want to trade in this account on days when the market or a stock price tanks. Traders with margin accounts only, may want to hold off on trading if the stock or market turns bearish.

Another solution for trading declining stock prices is an options account. In order to trade options, you've got to be approved and have the minimum balance in your account. Yet another form for your account. Options won't give you a tick for tick movement (when the stock price tick moves up or down, the option doesn't move in the same increments or even at all). You could have a stock price increase 2 points, but the option only increased ½ a point. When you play options, you play the option, not the stock price. There are many good books, classes and websites on option trading, including www.writingputs.com and www.income-trader.com. If you have a service broker perhaps he or she may know a little about options trading.

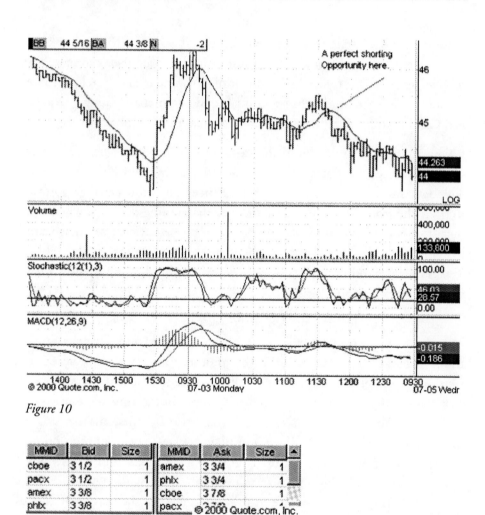

Figure 10

Figure 11

If you were to short the stock in Figure 10 at 45 1/4 you would have a tick for tick move as the stock drops in price. For every 1/8 point the stock drops it is another 1/8 point of profit in your pocket. The option quote however, includes time value. In Figure 11 you can buy the 45.00 put for 3 3/4. This may seem like a much easier price point to get into but because of the time value you are paying for on the option the market makers do not have to change the option price until the stock price drops to 41 3/4 (45.00—3.75).

If you're ready to trade, but not ready for options, then trade in a margin and short account. I will tell you that most professional short term traders like to only trade stocks and many of them only trade NASDAQ stocks. If you do decide that you want to position trade options then you may want to stick with strike prices with little or no time value. The one thing option traders have working against them is the time value of an option. You would like to get tick for tick movement in the option with the stock price. That means you should generally purchase two strike prices in the money and current month (front month). If you are an option position trader this should be common to what you are already doing. If you are not an option trader then please read up on options trading before trading options.

Your best bet for keeping more of what you've earned is through an Individual Retirement Account, IRA. Most firms will allow you to trade in your IRA. They will have some restrictions, but it's worth looking into. Consult your accountant as to the best possibilities for trading in a long-term account, such as your IRA and a mutual fund.

If you've started a business and are trading for your business, you certainly want to consult with your accountant on the tax liabilities and benefits. Perhaps you started a sole proprietorship and then later you decide you want to grow it into a partnership or a corporation. A good estate planning attorney can best advise you of the benefits and responsibilities of each. When you open a trading account, you will be asked if you will be trading in a personal account or business account. If you answer business, they will want a little more information.

Once you've filled out the paperwork, you may need to deposit some cash before the firm will approve your account—some cash accounts don't need money in them until you make your first trade. You will need to decide how much money to put in the account. I've said it before, and I'll say it again, "Trade with money you can afford to lose." Don't gamble the rent or mortgage money. When you play with money you don't have, you are gambling. Balance the numbers. Look at what the firm requires, what you can spare and what you can trade with to really make a profit in short term trading after subtracting the commission and margin fees. If you start with all your eggs in one basket, and later you are able to increase your account, move some of your new wealth into different accounts. You don't want all your money tied up in one place because you will always have a chance of losing it all if something terrible happens on a trade.

Here are some questions you may want to ask the representative or broker at the firm you are considering: If I call in a trade what is the average hold time? Ideally you want the answer to be, "you are never on hold".

Do you sell your order flow? Many firms engage in this practice and it adds one more step in the routing of your order taking up more time from the execution. You would like their answer to be no!

Once I am filled on an order how long will it be before I can find out my conformation? Three seconds or less is great but not more than a couple minutes.

Is there more than 1 way to place my order? Such as by phone or online.

How long have you been in business? Stick with reputable known brokerage houses.

How many stocks do you generally carry on your short sale list? Anything over 5000 is great.

What is your commission structure? With today's prices it should not be too tough to keep it below $20.00 per 1000 shares.

Can I trade both stock and options?

What is the average order turnaround time on a market order? It should be less than 60 seconds.

Will I have direct access to ECN's? This will help you to get better order fills.

So, you've decided you want to trade stocks and/or options. You've found a brokerage firm and/or broker that interests you. You may even have a mutual fund. How about transferring that over. Are you going to open a personal or business trading account? Perhaps you should speak with an attorney or an accountant before making this decision. Once the decisions are made, it's a matter of checking off on the lengthy forms, depositing some money and you're good to go.

CHAPTER 6

Market and Economic Indicators

In this chapter we will use financial reports as market indicators to help gauge the strength of the market and even help in deciphering the movement at the market open. Stock prices are part of our economic system. They are a reflection of our economic strength, our well being, and we have several items we judge the health of our economy by.

Market indicators

S&P (Standard & Poors) 500 Futures. Probably the best economic indicator you will find for judging the strength or weakness of the stock market are the S&P Futures. These are traded 24 hours a day with the exception of the weekend where they stop trading at 4:00pm eastern Friday and resume back up again on Sunday evening at 6:30pm. Without trying to turn this book into a book on the futures or its indexes (OEX and SPX) I will try to explain in basic terms how they affect the stock market. The S&P Futures are an options contract that gives the purchaser of the options contract the right to buy or sell a basket of stocks from the S&P. Throughout the day you might be able to purchase an option that gives you the right to buy a group of S&P stocks for $1300.00. If the S&P stocks were only worth $1300.00 then you would have parity with the option and no profit would be available to you. Now lets say that the stock market closes as it does each day at 4:00pm eastern and the group of stocks in the S&P Futures contract closed with a market value of $1300.00. Now that the market has closed some positive news has come out about a couple of stocks that are in the S&P Futures contract, maybe they reported positive earnings and or were upgraded by Goldman Sachs. We would expect this sort of news to have a positive effect on the stocks when the stock market opens up the next morning. Since the Futures are traded 24 hours a day they start to reflect the positive news right away and trade higher all night long. Lets jump ahead to the market open and see what happens with the market. At this point in time the S&P Futures are trading at a premium to the stocks price so at the open the specialists who control a stocks price will increase the stocks price to be equal with the amount of the S&P Futures. If they did not investors would jump in and sell the Futures contract at the higher price and buy the stock at the lower price to cover the sale. And they would continue to do this all day long unless the specialists raised the price of the stocks to meet the Futures price. So if the S&P Futures are trading up (above yesterdays 4:00pm eastern closing price) at the market open then we could expect the stock market to also trade up at the open. The opposite is also true. If the Futures are down at the open we can also expect the stock market to trade down at the open.

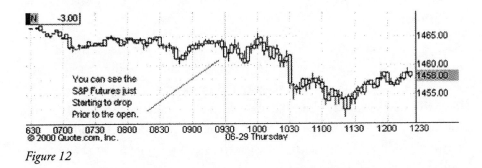

Figure 12

This does not mean that the market will trade this way all day long it only gives us an idea as to how it will open. How often have you seen the DOW open up 55 points higher and then be -47 points and back up to +61 within the first hour of trading? As a rough rule of thumb, the S&P Futures have a 1:8 ratio with the DOW. So if the Futures are up 8 points at the open then we could expect the DOW to open somewhere around +64 and if the futures are down 4 points at the open we can expect the DOW to open roughly -32 points. For every one point the Futures move we can expect the DOW to generally, move 8 point in the same direction.

For trading on the Nasdaq you can use the Nasdaq futures. A difference of 50 points in either direction should indicate a strong open up or down depending on whether or not the Nasdaq futures are positive or negative. Any number inside of the 50 point range will generally mean a weaker open. If the Nasdaq futures are only plus 17 points just before the opening bell then you can expect the Nasdaq market place to open up any where from + 1 to + 17. There is no exact number that you can divide the Nasdaq futures by to get the exact number the Nasdaq market will open up. Use the numbers as a general guide. You can find both the S&P Futures and Nasdaq Futures on CNBC premarket. You can also type in their ticker symbols into your real time charting software for a streaming read. Or you can type in their E-Mini ticker symbol (no extra cost for these) into your real time charting software. Both of these symbols change quarterly so check with your brokerage firm or charting software for the current symbol.

As a position trader you look to take small profits whenever possible, that usually means trading with the trend of the market. Follow the path of least resistance. So if you like to play the markets at the open you would look to buy stock when the Futures are positive and sell stock when the futures are negative. You can find the current Futures price on CNBC starting around 4:00am Eastern Time. It will be displayed in the bottom right hand corner of the screen.

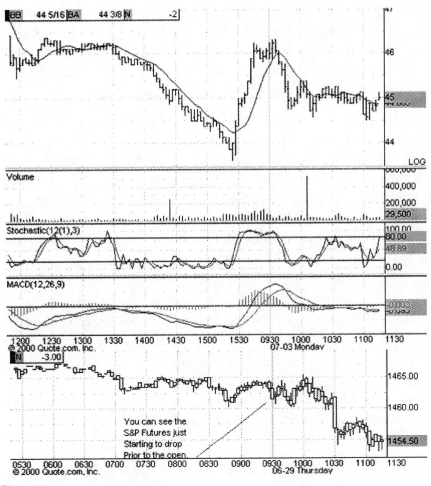

Figure 13

In Figure 13 you can see that the market makers tried to raise the stocks price at the open, but because the Futures started to drop just prior to the open there were no serious buyers and the stock dropped with the rest of the market. A great example of how to follow the trend.

While the S&P Futures are probably the strongest indicator a position trader will use to gauge the strength of the market, we will look at a few more that can be used in conjunction with the Futures to help in defining the open or overall strength of the market.

Bond Markets. If the Bond market is rising then the yield is dropping and if the Bond market is falling then the yield is increasing. If the yield is dropping then many investors and Institutional (Mutual Fund and Pension Fund) buyers will remove there money from a lower yielding Bond market and place it into the stock market where they believe that they have an opportunity to receive a higher yield. All of this additional buying has a positive effect on the stock market. And if the yield is increasing many investors and Institutional buyers will remove their money from the risky stock market and place it into the safer more secure Bond market. All this selling will have a negative effect on the stock market. The Bond prices change continually like stock prices. You can find the current yields on CNBC between 9am and 3pm. Many of your online brokerage firms will also carry these on their web sites. The most popular Bond yield followed is the 30 Year T-Bill. It is also known as the Long Bond. If you choose to follow this as I do you can either pay for an additional feed into your computer or follow the index TYX.X, which is the index for the Long Bond. You will find some powerful downturns in the Stock Market when the Long Bond nears or passes above their trading range.

Interest rates. When interest rates are lowered it provides companies with the opportunity to refinance their debt, giving them lower payments. It also allows companies to borrow money at reduced rates so they can purchase more equipment to increase productivity and grow their business. This buying also helps to increases profits on companies that sell these products. All of these changes are reversed when interest rates are raised. So an increase in interest rates tends to have a negative effect on the stock market and vice versa. As an added rule of thumb, many short term traders will not trade the market when Federal Reserve Chairman, Alan

Greenspan, is speaking at a conference. Whenever he speaks you will generally find it telecast live on CNBC.

A good way to play rate changes is to have a list of stocks from the financial sector. In this list you should have 3-5 financial stocks that are in an uptrend and 3-5 financial stocks that are in a downtrend. While watching CNBC and listening to the Fed Reserve Chairman speak you should have an order ready to be placed to either buy long stock or sell short stock depending on what he has to say. If he raises the interest rates immediately short a financial stock that is in a downtrend and if he lowers the rates immediately buy a financial stock that is in an uptrend. Do not hang around long. Take a quick profit and get out.

Strong Dollar. Another positive push for our markets would be a weaker dollar against the Yen or Euro dollar. A weaker US dollar helps to make US made products more attractive to overseas buyers creating more buying opportunities of American made products. More sales equal more chances of increased profits and higher stock prices. The opposite is also true for a strong dollar, as overseas buyers will shy away from American made products in favor of less expensive products. These lower sales could result in less profit and lower stock prices. This all by itself will not have a huge impact on the stock market but combined with other indicators it will help to define your trading strategy for the day.

Market Leaders. Although many of you new to the field of short term trading might think that the stock market opens at 9:30am Eastern Time you are not entirely correct. It is true that the NYSE and AMEX markets open at 9:30 but the NASDAQ market opens a little earlier. Since the NASDAQ market place is all electronically traded there is no bell to ring to start the trading day as there is on the NYSE floor. Approximately 45 minutes before 9:30am you can start to watch NASDAQ stocks trade as the market makers firm up and jockey for position. If you happen to trade with a SOES (small order execution system) you too will have the ability to trade pre and post market. Many of these orders are placed via Instinet, an electronic communications network that goes by the symbol of INCA on a level II screen. If you are trying to gauge the open you will want to look at the market leaders, DELL, INTC, CSCO, WCOM, YHOO... If these leaders in their fields are all down premarket then you can expect to see the market have a soft or negative open. The opposite would also be true. If at 9:15 dell was up $4.00, CSCO up $2.50, INTC up $3.25, and so on we could expect there to be a positive open to the tech sector. However if YHOO is down 3 points in premarket trading then you could expect the other Internet related stocks to follow their leader and have some type of a softer open than they would have had YHOO been up sharply.

I know that in most cases you will not get all these indicators going the same way but if your trying to gauge the markets and decide whether to go long or short in the morning on your plays it would be extremely helpful if the S&P Futures were up 8 points, the Bonds were stronger, yield lowered, the Fed Reserve Chairman had just lowered interest rates yesterday afternoon, the dollar was trading weaker against the Yen and Euro and all the NASDAQ market leaders were up in premarket trading. If you come across a day like this then it is probably not a good idea to look at shorting stocks on the open. Days like these are made for pure profit. Sit back and enjoy the ride. I have seen only a few of these days in my trading career and the market generally closes with the DOW up 300+ points and NASDAQ up 200+ points. As Murphy's law would have it, these will be the days that you over sleep or if you broke the cardinal rule, have all your money tied up in other stocks that you can't sell because you are down and don't want to sell at a lower price than you bought, so you watch the markets do incredible things and all you can do is watch. OUCH!

Economic indicators. We have looked at a few market indicators, now lets concentrate on some economic indicators. Most of these will be reported on CNBC as they come out. You can also find these on many financial page web sites with a calendar that lists dates, times and expected numbers of each of these reports. www.briefing.com has one that I find easy to read.

New Home Construction. This report is released at 10:00am around the last business day of the month. To play this strategy you will want to find a list of stocks in the residential home sector such as CTX, KBH, LEN and SPF. You might also look in the building materials sector for stocks like MAS, SHW, OWC, USG, and VMC. You will want to find 2 or 3 of these that are in an uptrend and 2 or 3 that are in a downtrend. As soon as the report is listed you will now be able to play a stock in a sector that will reflect the changes in the report. If new home construction comes out better than anticipated then you will want to buy long the stocks already in an uptrend as they will now benefit from stronger sales in their sector. And if the report comes out worse than expected then you will want to sell short the stocks that are already out of favor with the market and are in a downtrend.

Gross Domestic Product. This report comes out around the 3rd or 4th week of the month at 8:30am eastern time. Although there aren't any particular stocks to play with this strategy, it does help to set a tone for the market. It is to be used in conjunction with other market and economic indicators.

Retail Sales. This report is released at 8:30am eastern around the 13th of each month. It too can be found on CNBC or many financial web sites. To play this strategy you will work it similar to the new home construction report. If the Retail Sales report is to come out with expected growth of .9% and actually comes out at +1.3% then you can expect the larger better known retail stocks to have some positive pressure from a strong sector as these stocks will benefit on there next earnings announcement from better than expected sales the past month. These stocks might include WMT, DDS, FD, NOBE, KM, DH, GPS and FDO. To really get some good movements it would be an added plus if one of these stocks also had earnings coming out in the next couple of days and this stock also had a history of beating earnings or positive earnings surprises, positive news or even a possible split candidate. Since you have access to the exact date of the Retail Sales announcement from your economic calendar you will be able to do all your research the night before the report is released giving you plenty of time to make an educated decision as to which stock to trade. Regardless of whether or not any of these stocks have earnings announcements in the next few days or are split candidates you will still be able to find good quality stocks that are now in a hot sector. You would play the opposite if the Retail Sales report came out below expectations. Look for large retail stocks in a downtrend that have a history of negative surprise or have just recently been downgraded. Regardless of which way you play the report you do need to trade the strategy as soon as the market opens up and in the direction the market is moving. This means if the retail numbers are unexpectedly down you would like to trade large stocks in a downtrend on a down (S&P, DOW and NASDAQ open to the negative) day and vice versa on an up day. Try to get everything going one way and play the stock with the least amount of resistance.

The powerful part of playing the economic indicators is that you know which ones are to be released each day and what the numbers are expected to be. This gives you plenty of time to study the sectors to be involved with the economic reports. You should have a list of stocks you want to go up and a list of stocks you want to go down so when the report comes out you will be ready to jump into a profitable trade.

Oil Prices. If the oil prices have been raised it will have a positive effect on the oil stocks as they charge customers more for oil adding extra money to their bottom line. Their costs are fairly consistent and whether the oil prices are raised or lowered, it still costs the oil companies the same to pump it from the ground. Stocks who depend heavily on oil are apt to have some downward pressure when oil prices are raised. These would include forms of transportation like airline and trucking: LUV, DAL, AMR, UAL, CNF, YELL and WERN.

Quick reference guide

If the S&P Futures are strong & the bond yield is weak, the market should have positive pressure at the open. If the S&P Futures are strong & the bond yield is up, then interest bearing stocks should do well, banks and money centers. If the S&P Futures are weak & the bond yield is down then interest stocks such as banking stocks will be down & utilities such as SO, DUK, CSR, and FPL should trend up. If S&P's are weak and the bond yields are strong, then you're getting mixed signals. Find some other trades. Look for slams, earnings announcements, splits, IPO's, momentum or news plays.

CHAPTER 7

Technical Indicators

There are many books on technical charting that devote anywhere from 15 to 20 chapters on the subject. I would strongly suggest you visit your local bookstore or e-commerce book site and pick up a few books on technical analysis. We will discuss it here only to the extent of showing you some of the more popular indicators.

I can still remember my very first class on investing in the stock market. I was lucky enough to have two excellent instructors. Both were skilled chart readers and made stock picking appear to be extremely easy. I guess it was because of their ability to find and analyze good stock picks that I thought investing in the stock market would be easy. I thought all I needed to do was find the right stock and BINGO! How could I lose? As soon as I got home from my class, I devised a spreadsheet that had all the items necessary to obtain a good quality stock that would outperform the DOW and the S&P 500. I ended up with 30 indicators, including; increasing volume, recent resistance breakout, 4.554% retracement over the last 5 days and today it gapped open and closed at the high for the day… After all my calculations I found my success ratio to be only about 55%. Now as most of you traders already know, a win ratio of 55% really means that I was losing money (we tend to hang on to our losers and quickly sell our winners). So I added 30 more items to my criteria list only to find my win ratio actually drop to 50%. I could see here that I was working backwards, so I decided to eliminate all but the most important criteria for determining a great stock and soon found my success ratio up around 90%. I have read countless books on charting and stock picking and most of them fail to mention this one important fact. If you want to buy a stock and have it increase in price then it is a good idea to *ONLY* choose a stock that is *already going up!* How many times have you heard someone say that you are supposed to buy stocks on a dip? The one thing that they leave out of the sentence is the most important part. The dip should *ONLY* be on a stock that is in an uptrend and not in a downtrend. It is amazing to me how many investors will buy a stock on a dip in a downtrend, expect it to go up and then get upset when it continues to go down. The red sale tag is not a bargain if your buying junk. **If you want a stock to go up then, then start with a stock that is already going up. If you want a stock to go down, then start with a stock that is already going down.** It took me awhile to figure this out. Sometimes keeping it simple really is the solution.

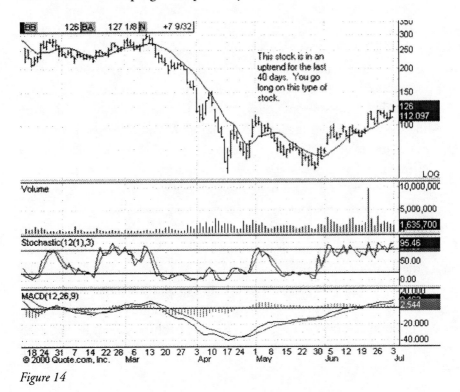

Figure 14

How to pick a trending stock. You can pick a trending stock by looking at the history of the stock price. Sometimes the trend isn't to obvious, so many traders will look for conformations from leading and trailing indicators to pinpoint entrance and exit points on trending stocks. One of the more common indicators is a moving average. A moving average is a trailing indicator, meaning it does not lead the stock price; it is an historical record of the stock price. A moving average is just what it implies, a moving average for a specific amount of time of the stock's price. If you have the ability, you will want to enter multiple moving averages on your real time charting software. When these two averages cross they indicate a change in pattern or possibly a buy or sell signal. When looking at a 1 minute price chart I will use a 1 and 3 minute moving average and when I am looking at a 3 minute chart I will use a 3 and 5 minute moving average. When looking at a daily chart, I will use a 30 and 40 day moving average. If you are able to use different time settings then try lengthening and shortening your time averages using 2 and 7 or 5 and 10 minute moving averages. If you choose too short of a time frame then, you will end up creating false entrance and exit points, and if you extend them too long, it might be too late to act on the information a crossover provides. Moving averages are only useful on up trending and down trending stocks. A stock trading in a sideways pattern will give too many false crossover signals from a moving average. The theory behind moving averages is since they are a trailing indicator they have to follow the past trading pattern of the stock. If you are using 2 moving averages on a stock trending up then the moving averages, which trail the stock, will be lower than the stocks current price. If the stock price starts to fall it will cross through the first moving average (M.A.) and begin trading under the first M.A. and above the second M.A. This is usually the start of a reversal. If the stock now crosses through the second M.A. then it is a good sign that the stock is no longer going to do what it did in the past. And since what it did in he past was go up, it will now probably go down. In Figure 15 you can see that in Mid March the stock dropped below a single moving average indicating the start of a reversal.

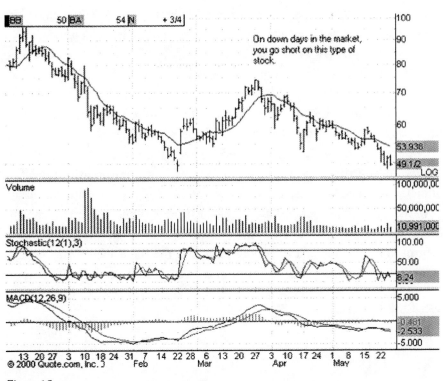

On down days in the market, you go short on this type of stock.

Figure 15

Support and Resistance lines. These lines are different from moving averages. These are straight lines drawn horizontal on the stock price graph for a sideways trending stock, and drawn at angles for trending stocks. To draw support and resistance lines first locate the lowest stock price and then look for additional low points that can be attached by drawing a straight line connecting the points together. See Figure 16. Next extend this line forward to use as a future resistance/support line. Now do the same thing using a high price and additional high points to draw your resistance line. The stock will try to trade in this range either upwards, downwards or sideways. Breakouts occur when the price is outside the support and resistance lines. Breakouts may be temporary and then the price will return to the trading range, or it might start a new trading range with new support and resistance lines. The theory behind support/resistance lines is that many traders will jump in on a pure momentum play while a stock is trending up. Some of these buyers are bound to buy in at a high point while others, those able to read a chart, bought in at a lower price. As profit takers who bought into the rally at a lower price take their profits, the trend will start to reverse its direction and head back down. Others who also bought into the rally who have not sold yet will see the stock starting to reverse direction, quickly sell and take their profits causing the stock to retrace back down at an even faster rate. The unlucky ones will be those left holding onto their positions and wondering how they will try to salvage their trade without losing any more money. Most, at this point, would be happy just to break even and be out only their commissions. So they place an order to sell at the point where they bought in, at the top, creating another point in the resistance line.

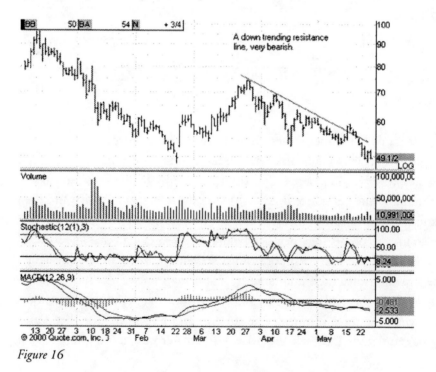

Figure 16

STOCHASTICS. Stochastics (pronounced stow-cast-icks) developed by George Lane can be used to help forecast future price moves. The two lines compare a stock's price to its past trading range. It tells us if a price is unsustainable and about to reverse direction. When a stock's price reverses its trading direction, it is called a reversal. Stochastics are plotted on a graph, with 2 lines, %D line and %K. Without going into too much technical jargon on how the %D and %K lines were developed, I will share with you how to read them. The best reversals will come when the %D and %K line cross and change direction close to the bottom or 0 line or close to the top or 100 line. See Figure 17. At this time, if the %D and %K lines are crossing near the 0 line of the graph and turn up, then you have a buying opportunity. A selling opportunity would come from a reversing stock with the %D and %K lines crossing at or near the 100 line and heading down. If the %D line changes direction first, then we will generally see a slow plodding reversal. If the %K line reverses direction to the upside first, as it usually does, then use it to enter into a trade when a stock is trending up and is on a slight pullback. The theory behind Stochastics is that together they represent buyers and sellers of stock. If there are more buyers than sellers then the Stochastics should be trending up and the price of the stock should be increasing. When profit takers head in and the selling starts to overpower the buyers then the Stochastics trend down. As the selling pressure continues, the price of the stock stops rising and then starts to drop. The whole process repeats itself when buyers think the stock has hit a short term bottom and buyers come in and overshadow the sellers causing the Stochastics to trend back up. As the buying continues the price of the stock should also reverse direction and head back up. The settings I have found most useful for Stochastics are: %K length 12, smoothing 1, %D smoothing 3.

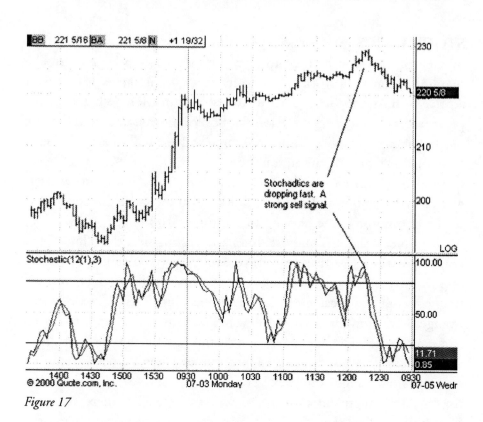

Figure 17

MACD HISTOGRAM. MACD (Moving Average Convergence Divergence, pronounced Mac D) is used as a broader measure of the movements of a stock. It should be used in conjunction with Stochastics to locate buying or selling opportunities on stocks. **A MACD histogram trending up above the centerline with Stochastics crossing near the 0 line and changing direction to the upside is used to find an up trending stock on a pullback. And a MACD histogram trending below the centerline with Stochastics crossing near the 100 line and changing direction to the downside is used to find a down trending stock for a shorting position.** The settings I find most useful with MACD's are: length1 12, length2 26, and for the signal line smoothing line, I use 9.

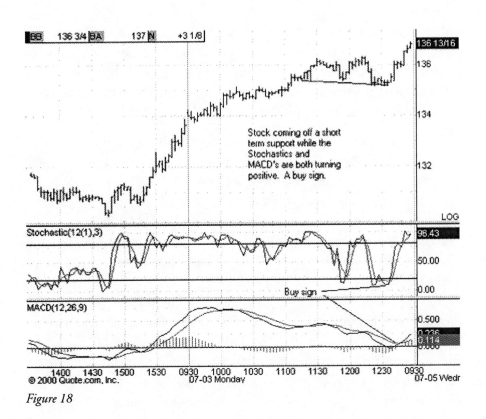

Figure 18

VOLUME. If a stock is to break out of a sideways trading range, it will need to have a steady increase of buyers or sellers. It is a bit like a jet building up speed for takeoff. Without enough speed (buyers for an uptrend or sellers for a downtrend) the jet is doomed for failure! A stock in an uptrend should experience steady or increasing volume. If a stock in an uptrend has decreasing volume, then you should be prepared for a reversal. If a trending stock is nearing a support or resistance line with increasing volume, there is a good chance it will build up enough speed for a break out run (breaking through resistance and continuing on up). If an up trending stock is nearing its resistance line and volume is dropping, then you should expect to see a reversal. If a stock exhibits unusual volume (8-10 times normal) and has a dramatic move associated with it, then there is always a good chance the stock will display a quick reversal as profit takers or discount buyers jump in. An example could be a stock that breaks out of a strong resistance line and the momentum, heavy volume, needed for the break out runs the stock up too far too fast, so a reversal comes as the profit takers take their profits.

RELATIVE STRENGTH. Relative strength is a broad term but can be used quit effectively in the market. In a nutshell in merely measures how strong something is compared to something else. I will generally compare a specific stock to its Index, the S&P Futures and the exchange it trades on. For instance, if I was watching and playing RNWK, an Internet stock, I would also be watching the IIX.X, Internet Index, the S&P Futures and NASDAQ. If they were all headed up and RNWK was also trending up then I would consider going long on RNWK. Another example would be for RNWK to open higher but the IIX.X the Futures and NASDAQ all opened lower. I would consider RNWK to have positive relative strength. If at some time during the day, NASDAQ, the Futures, and the IIX.X all reversed their patterns and turned positive I would immediately look for RNWK to head even higher because of it's strong relative strength. To put it in other terms, suppose you owned the only home in a neighborhood with indoor plumbing but home prices in your area were falling. You would expect there to be some type of resistance dragging the resale value of your home down. If for some reason the neighborhood prices started to change direction, increasing in value, your home, with indoor plumbing, would probably appreciate quicker than others.

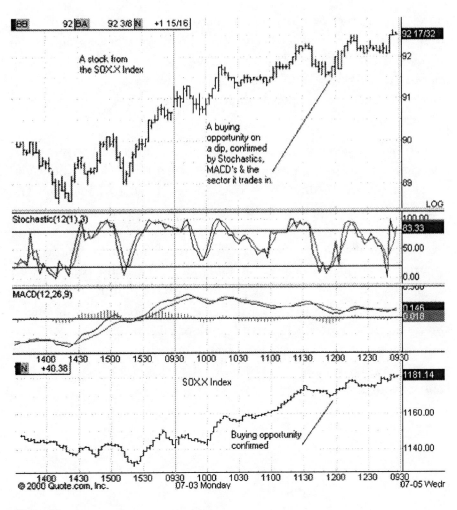

Figure 19

Another way to use relative strength is to compare price graphs of market sectors (Retail, Banking, Biotech...) to the S&P Future's price graph. Once you find a sector that is out performing the Futures you have a starting point. At this point you can compare the sector's price graph to each stocks price graph in that sector. For example if you found the Internet Sector to be outperforming the S&P Futures you would overlay the Internet Sector price graph over price graphs from stocks like AMZN, EBAY, RNWK, AOL, EXDS, YHOO… On up days in the market I will look to go long on strong stocks in this sector. On down days in the market I will look for weak stocks in weak sectors to short.

GAPS. Gaps in stock prices are fun to play. A gap is defined as a stock that closes at one price and opens at another. If CPQ closes Tuesday at $23.00 and opens Wednesday at $23.25, then it had a $.25 gap up. The nice thing about gappers is that more often than not, after gapping either up or down at the open, they will usually return to the same price that they closed at the previous day. When this happens, we will have an opportunity to play a reversal or jump in as the trend continues on through its previous days closing price. As a rule of thumb, when a stock gaps open and returns to the previous days close price it will do one of two things. It will hit this price and go up or hit this price and go down. *It rarely goes sideways!* Use the technical indicators to anticipate whether you want to trade in the reversal or the trend, and let the price graph confirm your decision.

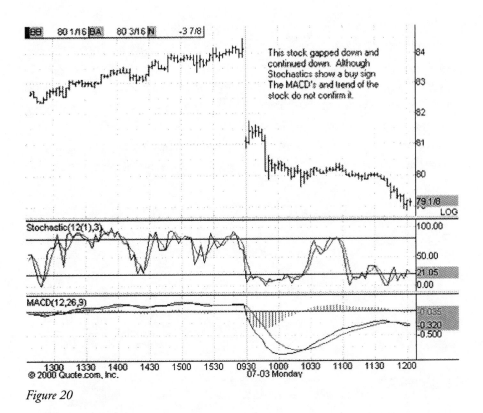

Figure 20

GAP and ½ hour Rule. If CPQ closes at $23 on Tuesday night and opens at $23.25 on Wednesday morning it has gapped open to the positive side. As a short term trader you would now use the $23.25 level as your new support line and use the $23.00 level as an old support line. If at 10:00 Eastern Time, CPQ is still above its gap open price and the Nasdaq market and XCI.X (Computer Tech Sector) are still positive and not dropping then CPQ would be considered a stock to go long in for the day. If however, CPQ has dropped past $23.25 and is still above yesterday's close price of $23.00 it is now a stock in limbo. This range between the gap open price and the previous days close is called "No Mans Land." When the stock is in this range it is best to leave it alone as there is no clear direction and the stock could reverse course quickly leaving you in an unprofitable position. If CPQ drops below yesterdays close price it is now considered a stock to short *if* the Nasdaq and the XCI.X are also negative and dropping. Of course you may still want to wait for the right technicals from the Stochastics and MACD's. The reason you will want to wait until 1/2 hour after the market is opened before placing this type of trade is to allow Amateur Hour to end. During this 1/2 hour period a stock can be extremely unstable and drastically change direction as the market makers manipulate a stock to take advantage of market orders.

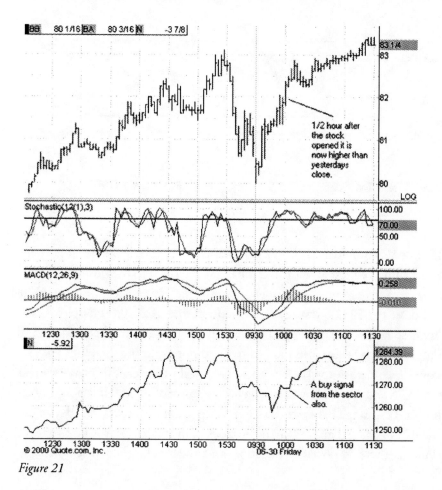

Figure 21

Closing At High On Strong Volume. Since most Institutional traders trade heavily at the close of day, watching the market and/or individual stocks in the last 1/2 hour of trading is a great way to gauge the strength of tomorrow's open. If there is plenty of buying and a rally going into the close then this may signal confidence in the market and a stronger open. If there is heavy selling going into the close then it may lead to a weaker open. You may have heard the term "Buy on Close Order". This refers to orders placed at the end of the day to buy a stock at the closing price. If you try to shadow the moves of the large Institutional traders (on a much smaller scale) you may find yourself without enough time left in the trading day to buy or sell the stocks that these firms are trading. This is where scanning software comes in handy. There are a few free services out in the market place that can do this for you but I have found none that are as easy and as fast as TC2000. www.tc2000.com. Here you can quickly scan for stocks with heavy volume that closed at or near their high. Because of how they closed on strong volume it would appear that there is some interest in the stock. Typically large Institutional funds like to do plenty of research on stocks for the long hall. They try to enter into a good growth or high tech stock. It may also be true that they are trying to pick up a few hundred thousand shares and were not able to get filled on their entire order. With this in mind, market makers will usually gap open the stock the next morning in anticipation that there will be some additional buying. Maybe the heavy volume has even attracted some individual investors who will also be looking at buying the stock the next day. Scanning for these stocks after the close each day will give you a potential list of gapers the next morning. If the volume is strong the next morning and the markets are positive on the open you will now have a gap open play and a list of stocks to trade.

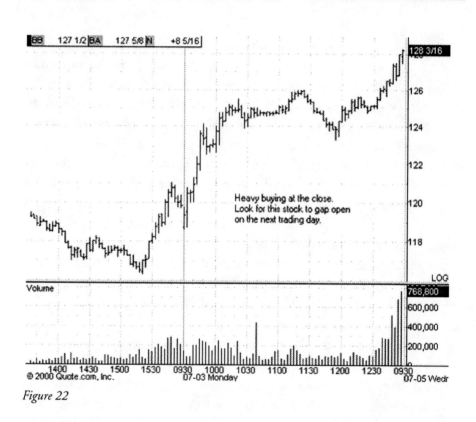

Figure 22

Trend Reversal Gap. When a stock gaps open to a higher price the market makers will fill orders and then try to buy or sell for their own account. Often this will result in a market maker fading the trend and reversing the direction of a stock. When this happens you will be provided with a strong trading opportunity called a trend reversal gap. Here is how it works. You are watching NITE, Trimark, and it closes on a Tuesday at $38.00. On Wednesday morning NITE gaps open to $39.00. In the first few minutes the market makers are busy filling all market and buy on open orders. Once they have sold their stock to all the buyers, sold high, the market makers will want to bring the stock back down to restock their supply, buy low. If the stock crashes back through the open price into No Mans Land and then through yesterdays close it is now considered a weak stock and one to short. This is a strong indication that there are not enough buyers to push the stock forward. If you are now lucky enough to have the market and or sector turn negative along with the stock you could be in for some great returns. The same trade works if the stock has gapped down the next morning and then rises back through yesterdays close. This is a buy signal. It means that the market maker gapped the stock down to take advantage of any sell orders so he could buy at a low price then raised the stock up so he could sell high. When other traders see this trend reversal gap to the positive side they see a strong stock that bucked the system and now should continue heading up. A buying opportunity.

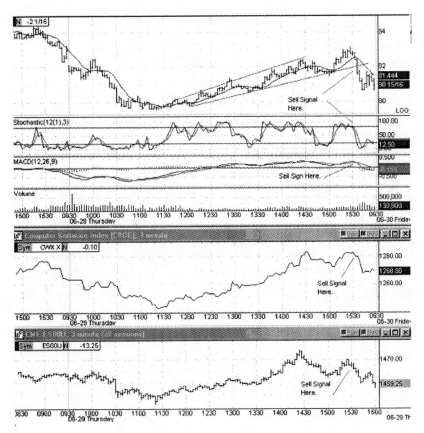

Figure 23

CHAPTER 8

How to Get and Trade on News

Despite what you might have heard or been taught in the past about market movements, it is news that drives a market. Good news, bad news, earnings news, upgrades, downgrades, news. News, news, news.

Many traders have the philosophy "It does not matter what stock I trade as long as it is moving up or down." This half statement has the ability to get a trader into some scary white knuckle type trades. The statement I like to use is "It does not matter what stock I trade as long as it is moving up or down AND I KNOW WHY." Suppose you are scanning stocks that are trading with heavy volume prior to the market opening. You see a 7 dollar Internet stock with an average daily volume of 76,000. This morning, however, it is trading at 14 dollars with volume already hitting 300,000 and still 3 minutes are left until the market opens. Excitement floods your senses as you start counting your expected returns. As you watch the trades roll by on your level II screen see the stock price hit 14 1/2 right as the market opens. Anticipation sets in! In a rush to jump in on the frenzy you place an order to buy 1000 shares at a limit of 14 1/2. Just as you hit the enter button the stock starts to run. You quickly cancel your order and place another order to buy 1000 shares at a limit of 14 3/4. Just as before the stock continues to run and you miss it again. The intensity is all consuming now as you cancel your order at 14 3/4 and place, in desperation, a market order to purchase 1000 shares. This one, you tell yourself, will not get away from me. You breath a sigh of relief as your order comes back filled at 15 1/4, 1/4 point above the current ask price. You settle back in your chair to watch the stock and see how high it will go before the profit takers jump in and turn the stock around. Just then you see a series of trades flash by at 14 1/4. You're already down $1000.00, FEAR!

Many of you, as you read this, can relate to this situation, as most of you have been here at least once. Lets now take the same situation and add a different twist. You are scanning stocks that are trading with heavy volume prior to the market opening. You see a 7 dollar Internet stock with an average daily volume of 76,000. This morning, however, it is trading at 14 dollars with volume already hitting 300,000 and still 3 minutes are left until the market opens. Quickly you type the stocks ticker symbol into your news provider (YHOO, Reuters, Equity Alert…) and find out that the stock was upgraded to a buy from an accumulate by the same market maker that underwrote the companies IPO 4 months ago. Next you look at a 3 month chart and see that the stock has been in a downtrend for the past 12 weeks. You look at the S&P Futures, traded 24 hours a day and a good barometer of market sentiment, and see that they are down 9 points with 60 seconds before the market opens. You then look at the Nasdaq Futures and see that they are down 48 points. Finally you gauge the strength of the Internet sector by looking at three to five Internet market leaders to see how they are trading. AMZN, EBAY and YHOO, RNWK… are all trading below their previous days closing price.

Within 3 minutes you have been able to gather information on a "Gap and Trap." A market maker makes money two ways. By playing the spread (buying at the bid and selling at the ask) and buying low and selling high. In our example the market maker was buying low and selling high. He just did it backwards, selling high and then buying low. Knowing what the market maker was up to would allow you to shadow (copy) him and short sell the stock at the open and when it dropped back down buy it back to close out your position. By taking a few extra seconds and looking up the news that pushed this stock up in premarket trading you would have been able to avoid buying long at the open and save yourself the feeling of fear that comes as a stock you are long drops, leaving your account down $1000.00 in 60 seconds.

Here are just a few examples of some news plays to watch out for or seek out.

Upgrades and Downgrades Major brokerage firms employ analysts to follow stocks and make recommendations for their clients. The bigger the company the more weight a buy or sell recommendation carries. Take as an example an analyst, working for Merrill Lynch, comes out and upgrades CPQ to a strong buy from a buy, citing stronger than expected sales this quarter and increased profit levels. This analyst then passes the upgrade along to all the Merrill Lynch brokers who then call their clients and recommend that they buy CPQ for their portfolio. With the tens of thousands of clients that Merrill Lynch has, including Institutional investors, it could spark a buying rally sending the stock to new highs. Also if the analyst is known and respected around Wall Street then some brokers from different companies may also recommend to their clients that they also purchase CPQ at its current price. These upgrades or downgrades most often are announced prior to the market opening. Because it is news that pushes a stocks price up or down we can also expect to see the stocks price change prior to the markets open. So if CPQ closed the previous day at 27.00 then there is a good chance that it will open up above 27.00 possibly at 27 1/2 or more. You might think that it is too late to play CPQ as it already gapped up on the open but the play still exists if the market is in your favor. The reason it is not to late is because of Rule #4 (listed on the following page). The stock needs to be in an uptrend. It is true that the stock will most likely gap up at the open but because it was already moving up without the upgrade it should continue in its previous pattern. If you are concerned about the gap and think the stock will pull back then consider using this strategy with the Gap Open 1/2 Hour Rule discussed in Chapter 7.

The items needed for a successful play are: An upgrade by a big brokerage firm, A high volume stock (the more volatile the better), The stock should be in an uptrend for the past few months, And the S&P Futures, for an NYSE stock, should open higher than 8 points to the upside. If it is a Nasdaq stock then the Nasdaq Futures should be up more than 50 points to the upside. In order to understand why this works I will try to explain each reason.

1) **The Stock Needs To Be Upgraded.** It is not necessary to know what is was upgraded to i.e. Strong buy, Near Term buy, Accumulate… only that it was upgraded. What we are looking for here is news. The upgrade itself is the news we want.

2) **Upgrade By A Large Brokerage House.** The larger the brokerage house the more weight an upgrade carries. Some of the larger brokerage houses are: Merrill Lynch, Goldman Sachs, Lehman brothers, Hambrecht & Quist, Bear Stearns, Morgan Stanley Dean Witter, and Deutche Bank Alex Brown…As a general rule of thumb "If you have heard the brokerage house name before then it is probably a larger house." You just don't want to follow a small brokerage house as they upgrade and recommend a stock to both of their clients.

3) **A High Volume Stock.** The more volume the better. We want this to be a stock that is watched and traded heavily everyday, even without an upgrade. Now that it has been upgraded even more investors and traders should take notice of the stock. The more buyers, the better chance it has of increasing in price. If the volume is too low then there is a good chance that a Market Maker or Specialist will have an opportunity to manipulate the price. Anything with volume over one million should be OK. Five million is even better.

4) **The Stock Should Be In An Uptrend.** You want the stock to be moving in an upward trend even before the upgrade was announced. This

will help it to move even further faster as traders will see an upgrade on a stock that was already moving in a direction that will benefit their portfolio. If a large brokerage house upgraded the stock when it was already looking good then there must still be some room for it to continue growing. There is no exact answer for how long the uptrend needs to be in place for, but if it has been trending for at least the last 30-60 days then it should be fine.

5) **Futures In Positive Territory.** See Chapter 6 for commentary on how Futures prices affect the market open. S&P Futures greater than or equal to 8.00 for NYSE stocks and Nasdaq Futures greater than or equal to 50 for Nasdaq stock. This would indicate a positive day in the market. If you are going to go long on a stock it is helpful to have the markets going up and not down.

The same strategy can also be used if the market place looks like it will open down but you need to make a slight adjustment to the rules.

1) **The Stock Needs to Be Downgraded.** This needs to be from a buy to hold. A strong buy to a buy is not enough bad news to work. It needs to be a hold or sell recommendation.

2) **Downgraded By A Large Brokerage House.** Same rule applies here as it does above.

3) **A High Volume Stock.** Same rule applies here as it does above.

4) **The Stock Should Be In A Downtrend.** A downtrend for the last 30-60 days is sufficient. A longer time frame is even better.

5) **Futures In Negative Territory.** This time we are looking for the S&P Futures to be down 8.00 or more points for a NYSE stock and the Nasdaq Futures to be down more than 50.00 points for a Nasdaq stock.

In this case when the Futures are down and the stock is trending down and then it gets downgraded it is like the nail in the coffin as traders who were holding on for some hope that the stock will head back up are now forced to sell before the stock hits bottom.

Now not everyday will you get the futures to be up or down quite this much so in the case where the Futures open up slightly flat there is still another variation to this play.

1) **Futures Are Up Only Slightly.** When the S&P Futures are up only from +1 to +7 for NYSE stocks or when the Nasdaq Futures are up +5 to +45 you will want to bypass individual upgrades and look for stocks trading in the same sector.

2) **Look For Two Or More Stocks In The Same Sector To Be Upgraded.** If you try to play a single stock that was upgraded on a flat day the chances of your stock gapping open and falling back down are great. You do not want to play one of these stocks. Instead you want to find two or more different stocks from the same sector that were upgraded. It can be by different analysts but it needs to be the same sector. This will create some interest in a sector and will carry over to other stocks in the sector.

3) **Choose A Different Stock From The Same Sector That Was Already In An Uptrend.** The positive news from the other stocks will create some interest in the sector. You want to find another stock from this group that was already doing well. Other traders will also look for this stock and trade it, as it was not one that will gap open. The good news on the same sector however, will help to push your new stock up.

4) **The Upgrades Should Come From At Least One Large Firm.** It is not necessary for both upgraded stocks to come from large firms as long as one does. Just the fact that two different firms upgraded stocks from the same sector will be enough.

5) **The Stock You Choose Should Have Good Volume.** The stock you do decide to buy should have good volume indicating that there was some good interest buy larger buyers. Anything over 1 million shares per day should be fine.

Just like before you can also adapt this strategy for days when the Futures are also slightly down. Follow the same rules but reverse them for down trending stocks in a downgraded sector.

Earnings. Knowing that a stock has some buying or selling pressure associated with it can help you determine which way to play the stock. If a stock has some potential good news coming to it in the next few days then their could be some traders jumping the gun and buying the stock in hopes that it will deliver on the news and jump up in price rewarding those who took the risk buy buying early. One of the more common plays of this type is an earnings run. Stocks that have a history of positive earnings announcements show up on trader's screens every quarter. These stocks generally have some buying momentum going into the date of the earnings announcement. If you are going to go long on a stock, it does not hurt to have other traders going long on it also. The market makers know all to well the earnings run play and will typically increase the price of the stock just prior to its release. When playing an earnings run strategy there are some helpful rules to follow.

1) **The Stock Should Have A History Of Positive Consecutive Earnings Announcements.** The more often a stock announces a positive earnings surprise the more likely it will do so again. MSFT for example has a history of announcing a positive earnings surprise and then immediately issues a press statement that the next quarter will not be so good. Analysts will go back and lower their projections for the stock only to have MSFT beat the number again next quarter. Also, if a company has good management in place that knows how to grow profits and cut costs (beat estimates) there is a strong chance that they can deliver another good quarter and reward their shareholders with an increase in share price. There are many web sites that you can check into to see the earnings surprises both to the upside and downside. One that I like to use is www.justquotes.com. Type in a ticker symbol, hit enter and then click on earnings growth/history.

2) **It Should Have At Least One Upgrade In The Two Weeks Prior To The Earnings Announcement.** Analysts have a job just like the average worker. They are graded on their performance and are always looking for a promotion and raise to bigger companies. A new analyst may start out on two or three small stocks and try to work up to the GE's and MSFT's. To do this they are graded on how accurate their forecasts are on the stocks and sectors they follow. The closer they are the better their promotions and their pay. In order to follow a stock and set the forecasts for the quarter and year performance, an analyst will keep in contact with the CEO and CFO of a company. CEO's, and CFO's are usually happy to work with the analysts as a strong buy rating can help boost their companies share price. So when it comes down to earnings time the CEO and CFO will want to try and steer the analyst to the proper numbers. Without giving out insider information a CEO can say something like, "We seem to have had an excellent quarter as sales have been up 3% from our projected figures and we have been able to switch manufacturers and save another 2.5% on labor costs." With this information the analyst can go back and recalculate the expected earnings numbers. If the stock then announces a positive earnings surprise the analyst looks good to his upper management and the stock does well as an upgrade and a positive earnings announcement help push the stock up. So when you see a stock that was recently upgraded just before an earnings announcement it carries some good news as to the expected outcome of the earnings. If the stock has multiple upgrades then chances are better that it will announce to the upside.

3) **The Stock Should Be Already Trending Up.** The fact that the stock is already in an uptrend will confirm that the stock is doing well. If large Institutions are buying the stock then there is some consensus in the market place that the stock is on track to perform well.

4) **The Whisper Number Should Be Higher Than The Estimate.** A whisper number is the expected earnings number for a stock that is circulated by traders, analysts and brokers. It is not a firm number that

anyone will commit to in writing but instead, a general consensus of what it could do. The number is passed around and given to clients as what the stock could announce. A great site for these numbers is www.earningswhispers.com. If the whisper number is higher than the actual estimate then there is a feeling that the stock will announce an upside earnings surprise.

5) **Trade Earnings Run Candidates Only On Up Days In The Market.** An up day in the market can only help your trading if you are going long on a stock. It is just a little extra wind to your back to help push you forward. Trying to go long on a stock when the market is falling is not a good trading style.

6) **Trade Earnings Run Candidates 2-3 Days Prior To The Announcement.** Your best luck with this type of play will be 2-3 days before the announcement. Going out further in advance will open you up to too many distractions. Traders will want to own the stock before the announcement and will look to pick it up just before earnings are released. *Do not hold the stock through the announcement!* Too often a stock will sell off on the announcement as traders who have profited from the earnings run sell and take their profits.

To find out which stocks are coming up on earnings announcements you can go to www.earningswhispers.com or www.fool.com and type in earnings calendar in the search box. Just like most other strategies you can also work this one in reverse. If the markets are trading down then you can look for stocks trending down with a history of flat or negative earnings announcements and with analysts' downgrades instead of upgrades.

CHAPTER 9

How to Trade Slams

One of my favorite strategies to play is called Point Losers, or more commonly known as Slams. A slam is defined as any stock that drops more than 10% in one day. An example would be CSCO trading at 100 dollars on a Tuesday and on Wednesday it is trading at 90 dollars. The stock is down 10 dollars for a 10% drop in one day. The reasons for this can vary quite a bit so we will cover them in detail later in this chapter

In order to understand how to trade this strategy I would like to draw you a mental picture. Suppose you took a baseball in your hand and with all your might you throw it onto a hard cement floor. What would you expect the baseball to do as soon as it hit the floor? Hit the floor and roll or bounce? Hopefully you said bounce, if you didn't then please do not attempt to trade this strategy. If you did get it then I have just showed you a way to trade profitably enough to quit your job! You can walk into work on Monday morning and let your boss know that you *have* to quit. You can no longer afford to work each day! Now of course at this point in your short term trading training I am kidding, but with some practice and some paper trading this could well be the one you retire with.

Everyday there are stocks that are winners and losers in the stock market. They are titled Biggest Dollar Gainers and Biggest Dollar Losers and Biggest % Gainers and Biggest % Losers. I like to trade the Biggest Dollar Losers since the Biggest % Losers generally show smaller stocks (I am looking for big companies with big volume). These can be found each day in just about any local newspaper that carries a financial section. They are usually found on page 2 of the financial section. You can also find them on many financial websites under the heading of Most Actives.

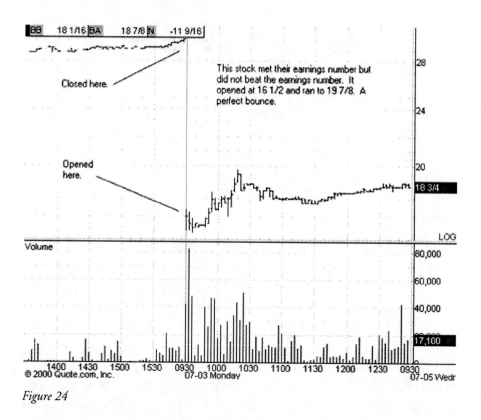

Figure 24

There are 6 rules that I follow when trading Slam Plays, I will list all 6 and then go back and explain each one.

1) **The stock must drop at least 10% on the previous trading day. The higher the price of the stock the better.**
2) **Volume should be above 500,000 shares traded on a daily basis.**
3) **The stock should not be trading at a 52 week high.**

4) The reason for the slam should not be associated with bad news.
5) Would like to see a slight up tick during last ½ hour of trading.
6) The trade needs to happen close to the opening bell and follow the Futures.

Now that you have the rules let's go back and explain in detail their meaning.

1) The stock must drop at least 10% on the previous trading day. The higher the price of the stock the better.
Ideally it is best to have a stock in the range of 50.00 or higher, as a 10% drop would then be a 5.00 loss. To really get your heart pumping it is nice to see a 100.00 stock drop 10% or more. What you don't want to use are the 6.00 stocks that drop 60 cents. They might bounce at the opening bell to the amount of 15 cents. On average I have found that a drop of 10% on no bad news will cause a bounce of 20% to 25% of the amount slammed. Lets go back to our original example. CSCO drops from 100.00 to 90.00 in one day, on no bad news, a 10% slam. The next morning I would expect CSCO to bounce 20% of its 10.00 drop or about 2.00.

2) Volume should be above 500,000 shares traded on a daily basis.
We want to follow the higher volume stocks, as these are the ones that are also followed by major analysts. In order for the bounce to occur there needs to be a large amount of buying at the open. We better our odds with a high volume stock. If interest (buying of a stock) was prominent before a slam it will dramatically increase after a slam as the perception of the stock is that it is now on a blue light special, thus bringing in buyers and creating a bounce. Stay away from the low volume stocks, 100k, and under. These can be easily manipulated in price by the market makers.

3) The stock should not be trading at a 52 week high.
Institutional buyers, pension and mutual funds regularly buy and sell stocks throughout the year. They purchase a stock based on future valuation of a stocks price, hoping to pick up a stock at 43 dollars and selling it when it reaches a price target that they are happy with, maybe 72 dollars. The

problem that comes up with this type of scenario is that Institutional buyers generally buy and sell a few hundred thousand shares at a time. Suppose you bought 500 shares of a stock at 43 dollars and unknown to you the UAW union pension fund also picked up 750,000 shares around 43 dollars a share. For the past few months your stock has been on a steady climb to the heavens and has now reached 72 dollars per share. You are feeling triumphant that you now control an uncanny ability to pick only winners. Later that night you log onto your computer only to find out that your stock was one of the Biggest Dollar Losers for the day closing at 63 dollars, down 9 on the day. Frantic to find an answer for the drop you search all your news sources but can find no reason for the drop. All you can find is unusually heavy volume on your stock. Thinking that something is up and not knowing the true reason for your stocks plummet you decide to sell at tomorrow's open price of 62 3/4 and lock in a 19 1/4 point profit. Your profit taking action along with the thousands of other investors who also bought in the low 40 an 50 dollar range continues to flood the market with sell orders dropping the stock even further the next day. This profit taking would not have happened if the stock were in its mid range. If a stock's 52 week high is 70.00 and its 52 week low is 40.00 then you do not want to play stocks that are near the 70.00 dollar price. It is best to play stocks that are at least 10% below their high, before being slammed.

4) **The reason for the slam should not be associated with bad news.**
Stocks can drop for a number of reasons, with each reason more and more difficult to decipher. What works best are the stocks that drop for no reason whatsoever. It might sound strange now but, yes, stocks do drop for no apparent reason. As you get better and better at this strategy you should be able to locate 1-3 stocks *everyday* that fit your five rules. Most of these will be sympathy plays, stocks that drop in conjunction with another stock, usually in the same sector. For all you engineers and mathematicians out there that find no logic in a stock getting slammed on the absence of bad news please remember that it is emotions that drive a market and not logic. Point in case,

AMAZON.COM had a market value of over 50 billion dollars and had never made a profit.

5) Would like to see a slight up tick during last ½ hour of trading.

If there is some interest in the stock at the end of the trading day it could indicate that the market place felt the sell off was overdone and might mean that there will be buying the next morning. This does not mean that you should also buy at the end of the day to take advantage of any gap play. Often times a stock will come out with additional bad news or downgrades after the market is closed causing the stock to gap down the next morning. This rule only pertains to stocks that got slammed at the open and you are trading them the following morning.

6) The trade needs to be placed close to the opening bell and follow the Futures.

Suppose that I told you that your local grocery store was going to give away 500 dollars in groceries to the first 10 people who walk through the doors Monday morning after 7:30. If you were hungry, would you wait until 9:00am to head down and see if you were one of the first 10? No, you would be there as close to the 7:30 mark as possible. Possibly even carrying an atomic clock to make certain that you were on time. The stock market is no different. Most traders will jump in at the open to capitalize on the blue light special being offered on the slam play. You wait too long and the bargain is gone. Remember the scenario of a ball that hits the ground and bounces? What happens after the first bounce? A second smaller bounce and then a third and fourth until it just rolls sideways. What we are looking for is a portion of the first bounce. Don't get greedy. This is designed to be a quick small profit play. Like most of the other strategies in this book you want to do this only on days where the S&P or Nasdaq Futures, depending on which exchange the stock trades on, are trading up. This will not work if you try to get a bounce when the markets are dropping quickly. The stronger the open the better off you will be at finding a stock with a chance for a bounce.

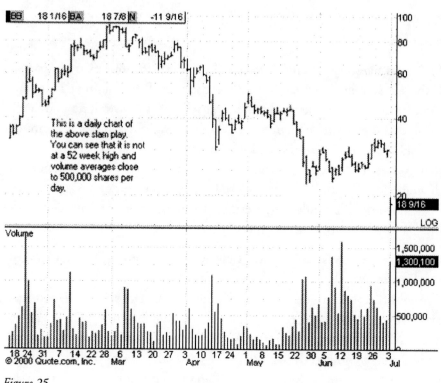

This is a daily chart of the above slam play. You can see that it is not at a 52 week high and volume averages close to 500,000 shares per day.

Figure 25

If you trade with options, look for optional stocks and play only deep in the money options. Two strike prices below the stock price is best so as not to pay heavy in time value. The larger priced stocks with a 10% loss are especially attractive when playing options because they should have a greater bounce (which is important because you won't get an exact tick for tick movement in the option).

This strategy works best on days that the market opens to the up side, Dow Jones, NASDAQ and the S&P open on the positive side. For days that the market opens down all you need to do is turn the strategy 180 degrees. Take a stock that *was* slammed on bad news that *was* at its 52 week high and short the stock as close to the open as possible. Remembering that bad news can last for a couple of months there is a good chance that continued profit taking along with the bad news will drive the stock even lower the next morning.

Unless you are an early bird, preparation for this play should be done the night before the market opens. This will give you plenty of time to research the companies before the market opens. It is also a good idea to recheck the news on the stock just prior to the opening bell. It is possible that some additional information came across the news wires while you were sleeping. Although it is emotions that move a market it is not how you want to trade. Prepare for your trading day. At the end of this section I've added a worksheet to assist you with your preparation. Do your homework and begin your trading day with knowledge and leave the emotion of trading behind.

SLAM PLAY WORKSHEET

Rule #1: The stock must drop at least 10% from the previous trading day. The higher the price of the stock the better chance it will have in a bounce.

Rule #2: Volume should be above 500,000 shares traded on an average daily basis.

Rule #3: The trade needs to be placed close to the opening bell and following the S&P or NASDAQ Futures.

Rule #4: The stock should not be trading at a 52 week high.

Rule #5: The reason for the slam should **not** be associated with bad news.

Rule #6: Would like to see a small up tick in the stock at the open.

Important items to remember:

Get in and out quickly. Take only a small profit.

If playing options, play deep in the money and with little time value.

If the market is down, the stock has bad news and is at its 52 week high, sell short or buy deep in the money puts.

CHAPTER 10

Where Does It Go?

My first stock market memory was filled with the sights and sounds of big city action, men in three piece suits and stock certificates. It was the early 70's and my family needed to sell some stock. After my mother signed the back of a stock certificate we headed up one of the cities skyscrapers to an office of stockbrokers. Once there, we were seated in an office with a view of the entire city. We turned our stock certificate over to a well-dressed man behind a huge oak desk and were told that the proceeds from the sale of our stock would be in our account in a few days. At the time, I believed that in order to sell our stock, our broker needed to call his clients and see if anyone wanted to buy our stock. If he were able to find a buyer he would make the transaction and deposit the funds into our account. Little did I know just how easy it really was to facilitate the transaction. Gone are the days of bonded stock certificates and traveling to the city to place your trades. Today's stock transaction can be done in a couple of seconds and the press of a button. But with this new technology, where does your order go?

In this chapter I will discuss some of the different exchanges and how to place trades on each of these. The oldest and some say the most respected exchange is the New York Stock Exchange, NYSE. Stocks traded on this exchange and the AMEX are called listed stocks as opposed to over the counter stocks on the NASDAQ. Each day on the NYSE floor there is an auction between buyers and sellers of stock. Orders to open and close positions are shouted out by members of the NYSE. These orders come from both individual and Institutional investors.

SuperDot

Here is the path of a typical order to the NYSE. You place your trade with your broker, your broker places the order to the NYSE via computer, the NYSE computer routes the order to SuperDot where it is passed along to a floor trader who will take the order to the trading pit for an open order outcry auction or SuperDot will route it directly to the trading post to the specialist who makes the market for the stock. Once there the Specialist will expose the order for all traders to see and facilitate the trade for the customer. Once the trade is complete, a transaction report is sent to the brokerage firms of both the buyers and sellers of the stock and to the NYSE depository for record keeping. Your brokerage firm will now electronically credit or debit your account for the trade followed by a trade confirmation to you. If this process is done entirely through SuperDot and bypasses the floor trader it can be done in as little as 20 seconds. Using a floor broker can add a few minutes to the order.

MMID	Bid	Size	Time	MMID	Ask	Size	Time
nyse	29 13/16	30,000+	10:54:26	nyse	29 15/16	45,500+	10:55:04
nasd	29 13/16	1,400+	10:55:29	chgo	29 15/16	2,200+	10:54:21
cinc	29 13/16	1,000+	10:54:02	bost	29 15/16	300-	10:55:29
bost	29 13/16	600+	10:50:37	cinc	30	5,600	01/01 00:
chgo	29 13/16	300-	10:52:59	phlx	30	500	01/01 00:
phlx	29 11/16	100	10:52:15	pacx	30 7/16+	100	10:55:07
pacx	29 5/16-	100	10:52:16	nasd	50	© 2000 Quote.com, Inc.	

Figure 26

Figure 26 shows the seven exchanges that trade most NYSE stocks. Each representing their best bid and ask price along with the available shares.

The use of SuperDot (Super Designated order turnaround) is a fairly new process for the NYSE. It was designed to help speed up the trading process. Nearly 50% of all trades executed on the NYSE are done without a floor trader and on the SuperDot system. SuperDot can carry trades of up to 99,999 shares at a time. Some of the benefits of SuperDot are its ability to link specialists directly with a NYSE member firm, and the priority it gives individual investors over Institutional investors. Using SuperDot, orders of 2,100 shares or less are given priority over larger orders. This helps to protect the smaller investor from quick price hikes. If a specialist is faced with a large Institutional buy order there could be an order imbalance causing the stock to jump in price before the smaller individual investor get his trade across. SuperDot bypasses this and matches up the smaller order first. With the use of SuperDot individual investors are able to route their orders, by way of their brokerage firm, to the specialist giving them quicker access and lower commissions.

Electronic Communication Networks

NASDAQ, unlike the NYSE, is open to all investors by way of ECN's (Electronic Communication Networks). These ECN's allow individual investors to actually make a market in individual stocks. It is not uncommon for someone sitting at home on his or her personal computer to hold the inside bid or ask on a stock. With the use of ECN's market makers and private investor's bids and offers are linked up and displayed on a national system for all to see and trade.

InstiNet

Instinet, the first of its kind was started back in the late 60's. It was developed for Institutional clients so that they could display their bids and offers to each other. These Institutions could then use Instinet to execute trades with each other. Initially, Instinet was used only for a select group of Institutions and did not allow brokerage firms or private investors to use the service. As time went on and SEC rules changed Instinet was opened up for all users. Large Institutions however, still gain an advantage in using Instinet. Block orders (Over 10,000 shares or $250,000) are not required to be posted on the system. This gives traders some misconceptions when looking at a NASDAQ level II screen. The Instinet platform, represented as INCA on the NASDAQ system, often trades 30-40% of NASDAQ stocks and a large majority of block orders. Most short term trading software used today, by individual traders, includes a button for routing orders through INCA.

MMID	Bid	Size	Time	MMID	Ask	Size	Time
INCA	110 11/11	5,300-	10:59:00	JPMS	110 3/4	500+	10:58:59
ISLD	110 11/11	1,200+	10:59:03	BEST	110 3/4+	500	10:58:58
REDI	110 11/11	600-	10:59:03	MONT	110 3/4-	100	10:58:22
NITE	110 11/11	500-	10:59:02	ISLD	110 13/11	700-	10:59:04
CWCO	110 11/11	100	10:59:03	REDI	110 13/11	400-	10:58:35
AGIS	110 11/11	100	10:59:02	NITE	110 7/8	200-	10:58:07
ARCA	110 5/8+	2,000+	10:58:51	HRCO	110 7/8-	100	10:59:04
MLCO	110 5/8+	200-	10:58:35	SBSH	110 7/8-	100	10:58:11
SNDV	110 5/8+	100	10:58:44	INCA	110 15/11	1,000+	10:58:52
WCAI	110 5/8+	100	10:58:36	BRUT	111	1,300-	10:58:42
RAMS	110 9/16	500	10:58:58	RAMS	111-	500	10:58:55
BEST	110 1/2+	500	10:58:53	DLJP	111+	200	10:59:03
MSCO	110 1/2	500+	10:58:51	MLCO	111	200-	10:57:49

Figure 27

Figure 27 shows a typical level II screen with market makers, their best bid and ask prices, their available shares and the time they posted their prices.

Island

Island, probably the best known and easiest to use for the individual trader, was started in early 1996. The Island platform, represented as ISLD on the NASDAQ system, is inexpensive and available to almost anyone with a personal computer and brokerage account. Datek Online, the backers for ISLD have created a simple way for any trader to trade like a professional market maker. Using ISLD allows traders to directly represent their buy and sell orders just as a market maker does. Saving you time AND money. Normally when you look at a quote you see both a bid and ask. These are known as the inside bid and ask (The best bid and ask price). If a stock has a quote of 26 x 26 1/8 it can be bought for 26 1/8 or sold for 26. This is where a market maker has an advantage over individual traders. They make

the difference between the bid and ask. This is known as the spread. With the use of ISLD your order to buy is represented as the bid and your order to sell is represented as the ask. Here is how it works. Suppose you are looking at ORFS, One Real Fine Stock, and it is currently trading at 26 x 26 1/8. Using ISLD you decide you would like to purchase 500 shares at a limit of 26 1/6. You place your order and now see the quote has changed to 26 1/6 by 26 1/8. You have become the inside bid competing against every market maker and trader in that stock. Simplified, the next time someone wants to sell ORFS, you become first in line to purchase the stock at a limit of 26 1/6. In a sense, using ISLD you become a market maker and buy at the bid and sell at the ask.
ISLD orders can be placed directly through Datek Online www.datek.com or on most real time trading software.

Other ECN's look to capture the ease and success of ISLD but are not able to match the availability and price. A typical ISLD order of 2000 shares or less is only 9.99 through Datek. Other ECN's charge a third party access fee when using their systems. Like ISLD, other ECN's give individual traders direct access to the markets. These include Attain, represented as ATTN on NASDAQ level II, Bloomberg, represented as BTRD on NAS-DAQ level II, Teranova, represented as TNTO on NASDAQ level II, and Archipelago, represented as ARCA on NASDAQ level II.

SelectNet
SelectNet, like ECN's is used to initiate a trade on the NASDAQ market between market makers or market makers and traders. The principle difference between SelectNet and ECN's is how the order is shown. An order entered through SelectNet is sent only to one market maker. SelectNet also allows the user to send an open order to all market makers at the same time, either way you use SelectNet, your order is not posted as an order to buy or sell on the NASDAQ level II system. This is called "preferencing" and is used when a trader wants to trade with a market maker but does not want to display their order for all to see. If a SelectNet user preferences a

market maker at the market makers posted price, then the market maker is duty-bound to fill the order at their current price. If the market maker does not fill the order and backs away from the trade, then they must show that they just filled an order at their current posted price and were in the process of updating their screen. A SelectNet order is a lot like a SOES order in that a market maker is obligated to fill an order at the posted price. Unlike SOES a SelectNet order is not automatically filled and must be set off by the market maker. A user might use a SelectNet order over a SOES order to get a better fill or hide their trade from other level II users. If you are watching your level II screen and see MLCO sitting at the inside ask buying up stock all day then you might think MLCO was a buyer of stock. If you see the Quote at 26 x 26 1/8 you might think that there would be a good chance that MLCO might buy your stock from you at 26 1/6 so you can preference him with your order to sell your stock at 26 1/6 and see if he wants to buy at that price. Your order would not be posted on the NASDAQ level II screen for anyone to see. If MLCO really is a buyer of your stock for the day then he can continue the trade and buy your stock at your price of 26 1/6. The trade would then be posted on the time and sales sheet. SelectNet is also used to trade with an ECN. If on your level II screen you notice a quote on ORFS at 34 x 34 3/16 and the order to buy at 34 is from ARCA then the buyer is not a market maker but is an ECN. Chances are that it is an individual trader using the Archipelago ECN to buy stock at the bid price. If ARCA is the only one on the inside bid and you want to sell to him then you must preference him to get the fill. Much of today's real time trading software will automatically do this for you by routing your order to the ECN.

SOES

SOES stands for Small Order Execution System and is a way to get an instant fill with a NASDAQ market maker who is displaying the best price on a level II system. The word SOES has been given a bad name in the past but it is really something that was designed to protect the small individual investor from the NASDAQ market makers. In the market crash of 1987 many traders were financially ruined because they were unable to sell their stocks while the market was dropping out. At this time the general way for a broker to facilitate your trade was through a phone call to a market maker. If you called up your broker and asked for a quote he would pull up the bid and ask on his screen and give you the current price. If a market maker posted 500 at a bid price of 67.00 then it meant that they were willing to buy 500 shares at 67 dollars. You then could instruct your broker to make the trade. At this point your broker would call the listed market maker on the telephone and make the trade for you. When the market was dropping quickly back in October 1987, many market makers were either to busy or unable to answer many of their phone calls and you, the individual, could do nothing but watch your stock drop in price with no hopes of selling to cover your now past due margin calls.

MMID	Bid	Size	Time	MMID	Ask	Size	Time
BTRD	110 3/4+	200-	11:01:53	ISLD	110 13/11	3,700+	11:02:09
AGIS	110 3/4	100-	11:02:07	INCA	110 13/11	1,800-	11:02:09
AANA	110 3/4+	100	11:01:46	ARCA	110 13/11	1,000-	11:02:08
MWSE	110 11/11	100	11:01:41	BEST	110 13/11	500	11:02:09
ARCA	110 5/8-	2,000+	11:02:04	JPMS	110 13/11	500+	11:01:36
REDI	110 5/8-	1,800+	11:02:09	RAMS	110 13/11	500	11:01:28
RAJA	110 5/8-	500-	11:02:04	AGIS	110 13/11	100-	11:02:07
BRUT	110 5/8+	500+	11:01:59	WCAI	110 13/11	100-	11:01:57
INCA	110 5/8-	100-	11:02:09	RSSF	110 13/11	100-	11:01:56
ISLD	110 5/8-	100-	11:02:07	NITE	110 13/11	100-	11:01:55
WCAI	110 9/16	100	11:01:10	DKNY	110 7/8+	500+	11:02:02
BEST	110 1/2+	500	11:01:59	FACT	110 7/8-	100	11:01:57
PRUS	110 3/8+	1,000-	11:00:44	HRCO	110 7/8+	100-	11:00:42
MASH	110 5/16	500+	11:02:08	BRUT	111	© 2000 Quote.com, Inc.	

Figure 28

On the above level II screen if you wanted to buy 1000 shares of the stock using a S.O.E.S. order you would only be filled on 500 shares of your order. The first three quotes on the ask side are ISLD (Island), INCA

(Instinet) and ARCA (Archipelago). All three of these are ECN's and using a S.O.E.S. order you are only allowed to be filled by a market maker. The First market showing on the ask side is BEST (Bear Stearns and Co.). Since BEST is only showing 500 shares on his quote you would only be able to pick up 500 shares at 110 13/16. Since S.O.E.S. has a time limit for another order at the ask on the same stock (See rule #2 below) you would now need to use SelectNet or and ECN to purchase additional stock to complete your order for 1000 shares.

All NASDAQ traded stocks are accessible through SOES and market maker participation in these stocks became mandatory in 1996. Buy orders placed through the SOES system are bought at the inside market makers ask price and sell orders placed through the SOES system are sold at the inside market makers bid price. Unlike SelectNet a SOES order, sent to a market maker, will be filled at the market makers current quote and lot size as long as the rules listed below are followed. The basic rules for SOES trading are a bit different then those on SelectNet or ECN's and should be studied before using a SOES system.

No more than 1000 share at a time can be traded using SOES. Lighter volume stocks may be limited to 200 shares at a time.

There is a 5 minute waiting period from each same security, same side trade. This means that if you buy, through SOES, 500 shares of MSFT at 65.00 and would like to buy another 500 shares of MSFT using SOES you must wait 5 minutes before you are allowed to place your trade. This does not however, stop you from using SOES to sell your 500 shares of MSFT or to purchase another stock other than MSFT. If you must purchase an additional 500 share of MSFT before your 5 minutes are up then you can use an ECN or SelectNet.

If you are trying to sell a stock short through SOES then you must wait for an up tick on the bid price.

If you are a Registered representative or a NASD broker then you are not able to trade in your own account with a SOES system.

Market makers must honor the lot size they are showing. This means that if a market maker is bidding 500 shares of MSFT at 65.00 and you SOES the market maker with an order for 1000 shares then that market maker is only responsible for buying 500 shares at 65.00 and not 1000.

CHAPTER 11

Your Competition

Many new traders seem to have the idea that position trading is an easy way to make some quick cash. The concept is simple, "if I am able to buy at the bid and sell at the ask price, just like the market makers do, then I can scalp a 1/16 to 1/8 point off every trade and if I trade in 1000 shares lots then I can make 60.00 to 125.00 per trade." Do this 10 times a day or 10 times a week and live the life that I was meant for. The reality of it is that most of these traders will lose a substantial amount of their capital, if not all of it, before they ever get the competition figured out. A smart trader follows the market in real time practicing trades without ever using any real money. If you are able to sit next to an accomplished trader day in and day out, and learn his or her secrets, it might make the difference in whether or not you are successful or need to go back and seek employment. It can be a humiliating experience to go back to the job you so ceremoniously quit only 3 weeks ago. Most good trading firms will allow you to place mock trades in real time within a phony account to enhance your trading skills. If after the end of one month a trader has not lost all of their money (trade these practice accounts with the same amount of capital you will put into your real account) and still has the majority of it left then they should decide if they want to practice for another month. If after the end of the second month they are now starting to make money, they have followed the market during market hours, pre market, and post market hours, continued to study and their practice account is starting to grow they can *then* decide if they want to go for the real game. It is disheartening to see individuals who have lost 40, 50, 60 or even 100,000 dollars of their life savings just because they believed they could make one more trade and beat the other players.

When a trader enters into a trade it is their hope that they will come out profitable and live to trade another day. It is also my ambition, professional market makers, professional traders, Institutions, and those of millions of other traders that we too will come out profitable and live to trade another day and enter into another profitable trade. Since it is not possible for everyone to win on every trade, why is it then that most traders, even start in the first place? In basic terms *trading is war!* In this chapter I will talk about specialists and market makers and how we as individual traders stand isolated in a foreign land surrounded by an enemy with seemingly unlimited resources. We may never be able to completely destroy this vast enemy but if we manage to win enough small battles we may be able to survive and prosper.

Every time you enter a trade you are going up against some of the markets best traders. These traders have the benefits of having learned the market economics from prestigious colleges all around the world. They then applied to a trading firm and learned the tricks of the trade from seasoned floor traders and market makers. Along with this experience these traders have access to their firms analysts who meet with the CEO's of the companies in which they make a market. Not to mention the financial backing of some of the worlds largest financial companies and occasionally some inside trading knowledge of large Institutional orders being placed and at what price these Institutions are willing to pay or receive for these securities. Knowing who these traders are and how they operate can greatly enhance your chances of coming out on the winning side of your next trade.

Your two fiercest competitors come from different exchanges: One from the NYSE, a specialist, and the other from NASDAQ, a market maker.

Listed market traders

Listed markets are those of the NYSE and the AMEX. Here there is one individual, called a specialist, who is responsible for making a market in a particular stock. This specialist has earned the right to make a market in a stock by demonstrating through past markets that have the ability to create a fair and orderly market without creating too much uncertainty in the stock.

MMID	Bid	Size	MMID	Ask	Size	
nyse	53 9/16	10,000	nyse	53 3/4	25,000	
pacx	53 5/16	500	pacx	53 3/4	500	
cinc	53 5/16	100	cinc	53 7/8	2,200	
chgo	53 1/8	100	nasd	54	100	
bost	52 7/8	100	chgo	54 1/8	100	
phlx	52 7/16	100	bost	54 1/4	100	
nasd	50	200	phlx			

© 2000 Quote.com, Inc.

Figure 29

It is this specialist's responsibility to match up interest or trades from floor traders and the computer SuperDot system and then decide which way the current quote should be moved. In the case of order imbalances the specialist generally covers the order from their own portfolio. There is only one specialist per stock and all orders go through this person. It would seem that this one individual might have too much power and insight but in order to create an orderly market they have the disadvantage of buying stock when there are too many sellers and selling their stock into rallies when there are too many buyers. And in the case of no buyers or sellers the specialist must still offer a quote and use their own securities to cover the trade. It is because of this reason that specialists are given other rights such as being able to set the price of a stock and seeing the depth of orders waiting to be filled. A specialist is continually rated as to how well they perform their market functions. If they let a stocks price fluctuate to much or do not buy stock or sell stock when there is an influx of orders then they can lose their specialist position in a security and even be fined by the exchange. If they do well they can gain further securities. Being a specialist can be quite lucrative and with securities such as KO, GE IBM and others there can be enormous profits for a specialist. So although it looks like a specialist has too much power, they under the watchful eye of the exchange do their best to make a fair and orderly market in their stock. A specialist has too much at stake to compromise their status and risk losing their position and possibly future securities.

An average role of a specialist might look something like this. A Coca Cola, KO, specialist would gather orders from the floor traders and the SuperDot system at his station. If he sees that a Merrill Lynch floor trader would like to buy 5000 shares of KO at 67.00 and the current quote is 66 7/8 x 67 1/8 and the size 3000 x 2500 then the KO specialist will change the new quote to show the Merrill Lynch bid. The new quote will now show 67 x 67 1/8 with a size of 5000 x 2500. This means that there are 5000 shares available at the bid and 2500 shares available at the ask. If an order comes through to sell 5000 shares at a limit of 67.00 then the specialist will match up the order with Merrill Lynch and facilitate the trade. If there are no other bidders at 67.00 then the quote will fall back to the next bid. In this case the new quote would go back to 66 7/8 x 67 1/8 size of 3000 x 2500. If another sell order comes in for 2500 shares then the bid price would then drop to the next highest bid. If the next highest bid was 66.00 with a size of 500 then the quote might look like this, 66 x 67 1/8 with a size of 500 x 2500. This is an unusually high spread and normally would not look this way. Generally the ask price would drop as traders are trying to get filled at the best possible price. However if the market was dropping and the stock had some bad news it is possible that there will be no buyers trying to buy the stock, thus the ask price would not be lowered. In this case the specialist would need to post a new quote using stock from his or her own portfolio to tighten the spread. The specialist might bid 500 shares at 66 ¾. The new quote would now show 66 ¾ x 67 1/8 with size of 500 x 2500. The specialist continually gathers bid and ask orders during market hours and updates their quotes when ever there is a new bid ask or bid ask size.

Over the Counter Traders

Unlike the listed markets NASDAQ stocks have many specialists for every stock. These NASDAQ specialists are called market makers. Market makers are generally large Institutional firms who trade for their own accounts as well as process orders for their clients. In each stock there can be anywhere from 1 to 40 or more market makers. Together they act as a marketplace each posting their own bid and ask quotes with the order size that they are each willing to buy or sell. Each market maker showing a quote is required to honor a two-sided market—be both a buyer and seller of the stock they are making a market in. This does not mean however that if GSCO (Goldman Sachs) is bidding 800 shares of MSFT at 65 that they are also offering 800 shares at 65 1/8. This only means that GSCO is willing to buy 800 shares at 65.00. In this case GSCO might be trying to buy 800 shares for one of their clients or for their own account. It might also be that GSCO is only trying to firm up the bid price and trying to give the stock some stability (more on this in the following chapter). In most cases if GSCO is really a buyer of stock their bid will usually represent the inside level II bid (the highest showing bid price) and the ask price they are showing will be slightly higher than the NASDAQ level II inside ask price. So the inside (best price) quote on MSFT could be 65 x 65 1/8 with a size of 4000 x 2200 but GSCO's quote might be 65 x 66 ½ with a size of 800 x 200. This means that GSCO is willing to buy 800 shares at 65 and willing to sell 200 shares at 66 ½. These market makers include firms such as GSCO, Goldman Sachs, MLCO, Merrill Lynch and SBSH, Smith Barney. These market makers as well as all other market makers list their bid and ask quotes on the NASDAQ level II system for all to see.

MMID	Bid	Size	Time		MMID	Ask	Size	Time
BTRD	83 5/8+	1,100	11:15:04		GSCO	83 11/16	1,000	11:14:32
INCA	83 5/8	200+	11:15:05		INCA	83 3/4+	2,000+	11:15:01
ISLD	83 5/8+	100-	11:15:05		MASH	83 3/4-	200+	11:14:48
CHIP	83 5/8+	100	11:15:05		SBSH	83 3/4	200	11:07:10
REDI	83 5/8+	100-	11:15:03		BRUT	83 3/4	100	11:13:23
WCAI	83 9/16+	100-	11:15:00		FBCO	83 3/4	100	10:58:41
NFSC	83 9/16	100	11:13:50		NEED	83 3/4	100	10:51:12
NITE	83 1/2	1,000	11:14:41		SELZ	83 3/4	100	10:48:20
SBSH	83 1/2	1,000	11:14:40		SHWD	83 7/8	100	11:13:56
BRUT	83 1/2	300	11:13:20		HRZG	83 7/8	100	11:13:40
MASH	83 1/2	200	11:13:56		PERT	83 7/8	100	11:11:10
SHWD	83 1/2	100	11:14:00		JPMS	83 7/8	100	11:11:02
MLCO	83 1/2	100	11:13:40		MONT	83 7/8	100	11:08:08
DLJP	83 1/2	100	11:13:11		MADF	84	500	11:08:06
MSCO	83 3/8	1,000	11:11:02		ISLD	84+	200-	11:14:59
HRZG	83 3/8	100	11:12:16		MLCO	84	200	11:04:25
JPMS	83 3/8	100	11:11:02		RSSF	84	100	10:48:07
MONT	83 3/8	100	11:08:08		VNDM	84 1/8	1,000	11:14:11
FLTT	83 5/16-	100-	11:14:52		MSCO	84 1/8	1,000	11:11:02
LEHM	83 5/16	100	11:13:21		PRUS	84 1/8	100	11:11:05
DBKS	83 1/4	100	11:12:19		BEST	84 1/8	100	10:51:35
SLKC	83 1/4	100	11:07:54		SNDV	84 1/8	100	10:47:46
FBCO	83 1/4	100	10:58:41		WARR	84 1/4	100	11:11:07
GSCO	83 1/8	1,000	11:14:32		OLDE	84 1/4	100	10:56:02
MADF	83	100	10:50:42		FLTT	84 1/4	100	10:44:07
RSSF	83	100	10:48:07		LEHM	84 5/16	100	11:13:21
SELZ	82 7/8	100	10:48:20		CIBC	84 3/8	100	10:35:35
OLDE	82 3/4	300	10:56:02		MWSE	84 1/2	500	11:12:02
PERT	82 3/4	200	11:12:13		TWPT	84 1/2	100	10:58:10
WARR	82 3/4	100	11:05:28		DLJP	84 9/16	100	11:12:48
COWN	82 3/4	100	10:36:42		NFSC	84 9/16	© 2000 Quote.com, Inc.	

Figure 30

When placing a trade for an over the counter stock, your broker has the ability to pull up the NASDAQ level II screen and see who has the best price listed and how many shares they are willing to buy or sell. The order can then be routed to that market maker by way of telephone, by preferencing them with SelectNet, SOES or through an ECN.

One of the major differences between the NASDAQ and the listed markets is the ability of the individual trader to act as a market maker and buy at the bid price and sell at the ask price. This allows the individual trader to pocket the difference between the bid ask price and make money with smaller price movements. For example let us say that you wanted to buy some TNMS (the next Microsoft) and it was trading with a quote of 11 ¼ x 11 3/8 with a size of 1000 x 1200. Using an ECN such as ISLD (the Island system from Datek) you enter an order to buy 1000 shares at 11 5/16 within seconds you will see the new level II quote read 11 5/16 x 11 3/8 with a size of 1000 x 1200. You are now sitting at the inside bid and represent the best available price. The next time someone wants to sell up to 1000 shares of TNMS you will be the buyer of the TNMS at 11 5/16. The TNMS quote would then fall back to 11 1/4 x 11 3/8 size of 1000 x 1200. Depending on why you bought TNMS you could either hang on to the stock and sell at a higher price or place an order to sell TNMS at the current asking price of 11 3/8. If you place an order to sell at 11 3/8 the new quote would read 11 1/4 1200 x 11 3/8 2200. If someone places an order to buy 1000 shares of TNMS you would then be in the running along with other ECN's or market makers to sell your stock at 11 3/8. Depending on how the potential buyer placed their order you may be filled first or anywhere up to last at 11 3/8. However if an order comes in to buy 2200 shares of TNMS then you will be filled at the same time as the other market makers offering their shares at 11 3/8. When all 2200 shares have been bought then the asking price will move to the next lowest price showing on the NASDAQ level II screen. When this happens the market makers on the bid side will usually move up their bid price to reflect the price change. The new quote might now read something like 11 5/16 1200 x 11 7/16 2000.

Market makers, unlike specialists, generally tend to police themselves. If a market maker who is required to honor a two-sided market is actively selling stock and their spread is too wide i.e. showing a bid price of 43 and an ask price 47 then they can be shunned from the market maker community and even turned into the NASD for fines or other disciplinary action. There is no set law as to how much a market maker must show on their spread but it is a generally accepted practice of showing somewhere close to what other market makers are showing. Thus if GSCO is showing a spread of only 1 ¼ points on TNSM and MLCO is showing a spread of only 1 3/8 points on TNMS then a market maker who is actively trading TNMS who is showing a spread of 2 ¾ points is not considered to be honoring a two sided market. Another violation that market makers discourage others from is called "backing away". If a market maker shows a quote and refuses to honor that quote it is referred to as backing away.

CHAPTER 12

Closely Guarded Secrets

Trading against professional market makers can not only be intimidating but can also be an unprofitable experience. Learning to watch and understand their movements can help you to recognize whether or not they are just honoring a two-sided market or are really buyers or sellers of large quantities of stock. Understanding this process is one of a trader's first steps to making a living in the market.

Most new traders are not aware that NADSAQ offers three different quote levels.

Level One (Level I) provides real time quotes with the shares available at the current price. These current quotes are the inside quotes only and are what many retail and online brokers use for their clients.

Level II is being used more and more often. Level II allows any trader the ability to see all market markers making a market in a stock along with their quote and size. As a snapshot this gives a trader the ability to see the depth on a stock—the number of market makers lined up on a bid or ask and how many shares they are bidding or offering and at what price. Watching a stocks level II screen on a continuing basis gives a trader the capability of judging the stocks support and resistance level along with its short term trend. Level II quotes are used by retail traders and most position traders.

Level III is like level II but is only used by the market makers. Along with the same functions of a level II screen a level III screen allows a market maker the ability to enter quotes and update or refresh those quotes as needed. If your goal is to beat the market maker at his game then you must learn to read a level II screen and watch the market makers to see how they jump from the bid to the ask and conceal their intentions from the uninitiated.

A level II screen consists mainly of two parts. A bid side and an ask side. The market makers lined up on the bid side are representing their intentions to buy stock at their posted price with the amount of shares that they are willing to buy and the time that they posted their bid. See Figure 31. The market makers lined up on the ask side are representing their intentions to sell stock at their posted price, the amount of shares that they are willing to sell and the time that they posted their offer. For a list of which market maker you are trading against go to www.nasdaqtrader.com and click on the symbol directory.

MMID	Bid	Size	Time	MMID	Ask	Size	Time
ISLD	61 5/16	14,600-	11:24:24	FCOL	61 3/8	1,000+	11:24:25
GSCO	61 5/16+	1,000-	11:24:06	WCAI	61 3/8	1,000+	11:24:23
SLKC	61 5/16+	1,000	11:23:28	INCA	61 3/8	400-	11:24:25
MASH	61 5/16	900-	11:24:02	REDI	61 7/16	1,500+	11:23:35
NITE	61 5/16-	800-	11:23:24	ISLD	61 7/16+	1,000+	11:24:22
MSCO	61 5/18	700-	11:23:18	PRUS	61 7/16-	1,000+	11:22:43
BTRD	61 5/18	500-	11:24:19	MSCO	61 7/16-	1,000	11:22:41
INCA	61 5/16	500-	11:24:18	NITE	61 7/16-	900-	11:24:12
MADF	61 5/16+	500-	11:24:13	GSCO	61 1/2+	1,000	11:21:37
REDI	61 5/16	500-	11:24:12	MONT	61 1/2	1,000	11:19:46
WCAI	61 5/16	100	11:23:26	MLCO	61 1/2	1,000	11:17:55
ARCA	61 1/4-	1,500+	11:23:19	KCMO	61 1/2-	© 2000 Quote.com, Inc.

Figure 31

The market makers are lined up from the best (inside) price to the worst price on both the bid and ask. On the left hand side, the bid side, the market maker who is bidding to buy the stock at the best price is placed on the top of the list. In a situation where there are multiple market makers bidding the same price the market maker who is bidding to buy the most shares will be on top. If multiple market makers bidding the same price and same amount of shares the one who posted their shares last will be on top. In Figure 32, the market maker ANNA is bidding to buy 4,100 shares of ATHM at 18 ¼. The next listed bid price is from the Island ECN ISLD. Someone using ISLD is also bidding 18 ¼ but only wanting to buy 1200 shares. The + next to the 1200 shares indicates that the amount of shares wanting to be bought has recently been increased. After ISLD there are two market makers each wanting to buy 1000 shares, SHWD and NTRD. Since SHWD posted his order at 14:45:18 and NTRD posted his order at 14:42:25 SHWD is listed first on the level II screen. Using this level II screen it is possible to see that there are 9 market makers wanting to purchase ATHM at a price of 18 ¼. These nine market makers also want to purchase a combined total of 8700 shares between them. However on the ask side of the screen you can see that only one market maker, PWJC is offering to sell 1000 shares of ATHM at a limit of 18 5/16. Once those 1000 shares have been bought the price will likely move up to the next offered price of 18 3/8. A quick scan of this level II screen on ATHM might tell you that there is good support at 18 ¼ and that most market makers want to buy this stock and not sell the stock. On a day when the NASDAQ is moving up, the internet sector, IIX.X, is moving up and if ATHM has been in an uptrend for the past few trading sessions then it might a profitable play to go long on ATHM.

MMID	Bid	Size	Time		MMID	Ask	Size	Time
AANA	18 1/4	4,100	14:33:44		PWJC	18 5/16	1,000+	14:53:06
ISLD	18 1/4	1,200+	14:56:05		PERT	18 3/8	2,300	14:41:44
SHWD	18 1/4	1,000	14:45:18		NITE	18 3/8-	1,000-	14:55:00
NTRD	18 1/4	1,000	14:42:25		MASH	18 3/8	1,000	14:43:14
INCA	18 1/4	700+	14:55:55		BRUT	18 3/8+	500+	14:52:25
NITE	18 1/4	300	14:48:43		LEHM	18 3/8	100	14:42:08
FCAP	18 1/4	200	14:34:17		INCA	18 7/16	1,000+	14:52:31
SLKC	18 1/4+	100	14:55:41		ISLD	18 7/16+	1,000+	14:51:46
PRUS	18 1/4	100	14:48:19		SHWD	18 7/16	200	14:43:04
LEHM	18 1/8	100	14:36:35		MLCO	18 1/2	2,500	14:01:25
FBCO	18 1/8	100	11:11:51		FLTT	18 1/2-	2,000+	14:55:35
RSSF	18 1/8	100	10:57:11		BEST	18 1/2	200	12:27:28
REDI	18 1/16-	1,000+	14:53:57		SEAB	18 1/2	100	13:12:53
PWJC	18 1/16	100	14:13:05		SBSH	18 1/2	100	12:38:53
MLCO	18	3,000	14:01:36		ARCA	18 9/16	2,500	14:45:32
BRUT	18	900	14:43:34		JBOC	18 9/16	200	11:12:25
MADF	18	600	14:25:41		FCAP	18 5/8	2,000	12:00:05
HRZG	18	600	14:06:08		JPMS	18 5/8	1,000	13:34:34
MASH	18	100	14:42:53		HRZG	18 5/8	100	14:27:59
MWSE	18	100	14:03:49		DAIN	18 5/8	100	11:12:14
DAIN	18	100	11:11:50		FBCO	18 5/8	100	11:11:51
FAHN	18	100	10:17:32		NTRD	18 11/16	500	14:37:21
HMQT	18	100	09:53:34		MONT	18 11/16	100	14:07:03
BTRD	17 15/16-	100-	14:55:35		RCAP	18 3/4	2,100	11:16:28
SBSH	17 7/8	100	11:51:55		DBKS	18 3/4	100	11:40:50

Figure 32

Using a level I screen all you would be able to see would be the inside quote of 18 ¼ x 18 5/16 with a size of 4100 x 1000. You would not be able to see the depth of buyers wanting to buy this stock at 18 ¼ or that no other sellers were offering to sell the stock at 18 5/16.

A level II screen is only as good as the person who reads it. Another tool to use when looking at a level II screen is the Time of Sales Log. The Time of Sales Log will help you understand if a market maker is really just fulfilling his role of creating a two-sided market or is really a buyer or seller of stock. For instance, if you see that market maker MLCO is sitting on the inside ask price on a stock and is offering 500 shares of stock for sale and the Time of Sales Log continually shows 500 lot trades being posted at the asking price and MLCO does not go away then it is possible that MLCO really has large quantities of stock for sale. It could be that MLCO has been contacted by a large Institution to sell 750,000 shares of XYZ stock. It is now the job of MLCO to sell the stock at the highest possibly price. If MLCO were to post that he had 750,000 of XYZ stock for sale then all other market makers on the bid side would immediately lower their bidding price. In this role MLCO is playing the role of the AX, the heavy hitter on a particular stock. It is not until you see MLCO disappear from the inside ask price that you can expect the stock to climb in price. So only seeing a level II screen without the use of a Time of Sales Log can be misleading and could offer a trader the wrong information on when to enter or exit a trade.

The Time of Sales Log, which is continually updating with each trade, should include the time of each trade, the price of each trade and the size of the trade. These two tools work excellent together when trying to decide the future movement of a stock. Don't be fooled however, in believing that a Time of Sales Report is always accurate. Often times a market maker will manipulate the trades to make money twice on the same trade. Here is how it works and how it traps the individual investor into trading into the wrong direction. One day as I was watching a market maker doing a terrible job of filling what I guessed to be a large Institutional sell order I decided to check around and see if there was some negative news that might be causing the sell off. I came across a stock market chat site where a trader who called himself Perfecto was writing a commentary on block trades on the stock I was watching. His letter went something like this "The stock which has a total volume so far today of 1.3 million, more than 2 times its ADV (average daily volume), has only had 11 block trades totaling 567,000 shares. This means that the Institutions have sold less than ½ of all shares today and individual traders have been dumping the remaining 750,000 shares. As we know that most individual traders trade in shares of 1000 or less that means hundreds or thousands of traders are selling off the stock today and I can find no bad news as to why it is in a sell off mode. What do all these traders know that I don't? Can anyone help me with this?" Normally I do not like to engage in chat sites but this fellow was falling for a secret most market makers don't want to share. I responded with the following letter. "Block trades are not always as easy to spot as you might think. Earlier this morning PIPR started filling what looks to be a sell order from a large Institutional firm. This could be a pension fund, hedge fund or even a mutual fund. At the open this morning PIPR showed up at the inside bid trying to buy stock. He quoted a size of 4000, meaning he wanted to buy 4000 shares of the stock. A size this large on a relatively small stock was enough to push the stock up in early trading. INCA followed right behind PIPR with a size of 3000. INCA is Instinet and can be used by both market makers and individual investors. As the stock was rising INCA also positioned himself on the inside ask and sold shares as investors bought into what looked like strength. Most investors saw large quantities on the bid side and assumed that there were really market makers waiting to buy the stock. In reality it was PIPR acting like he wanted to buy the stock when he really had a large order to sell. He was driving up the price of the stock so he could short it at a higher price. All he had to do was show the illusion that he wanted to buy the stock and that sent buyers into the stock. He had accomplished part of his goal. As other market makers caught on to what he was doing they also began to offer stock for sale until the level II screen had multiple market makers lined up in depth on the ask side of the screen. Individual traders then started to panic and the stock went into a free fall from there. Throughout the rest of the day PIPR was able to throw in a few head fakes and a wiggle or two to momentarily push the stock back up and sell again into strength. Towards the end of the day PIPR was probably able to fill most of his trades slightly above the VWAP (Value Weighted Average Price) and then in the last ½ hour he went to town and posted a large order size from PIPR and INCA on the ask side. This was the final nail in the coffin as buyers went away and the stock dropped another 2 points. Now that PIPR had sold 500,000+/- shares at an average price of 17

¼ and the stock was now at 15 ¾ he went back to the Institutional firm and told them that he had been able to sell and found buyers for all 500,000 shares at an average price of 16 7/8. He then starts posting his large block trades, to the Institutional seller, on the Time of Sales Log. This does not cause the stock to drop any further, or go up, as the trades really happened earlier in the day. What it does do however is show as two trades when in reality it was only a market maker fulfilling an order. So Perfecto, even though the block trades were only about 1/3 of the total shares traded PIPR filled those block trades in small 100, 500 and 1000 share increments. Both the small increment trades and the block trades show up on the Time of Sales Log but in reality they were both the same trade. A market maker will also do this throughout the day and disperse the block trades every ½ hour or so." My response was a bit more than the average user posts to a message board and I don't know if he even read it but I do believe that education on the part of traders is the only thing that will help us to stay in the game.

With the knowledge that a market maker has on large orders waiting to be filled he is able to front run a stock and make money in his own account while he fills his clients order. It may seem that this should be illegal as the market maker has inside knowledge on the unfilled orders and can use this to benefit his own account and manipulate the direction of a stock but the S.E.C. takes the stance that market makers are taking a risk in that the stock direction may change course and the market maker will be left in an unprofitable position.

The good news about block trades is that on the NYSE and the AMEX only one specialist fills the orders and is not allowed to front run a stock so when a block trade is posted there, it is usually accurate in time and size and accurate as to whether there really is buying or selling going on.

One of the more closely guarded secrets is that we, the buyers and sellers acting as a group, *do not* move a stock in either direction as we buy and sell a stock. In reality it is really the Ax who moves a stock. For every stock traded on the Nasdaq one market maker plays the role of the heavy hitter. This is generally the market maker with a large portfolio and controls huge lots of the stock in their own account. Often times the Ax is also an underwriter or lead underwriter and controls a large portion of the float (Outstanding shares of the stock). As a rule of thumb Institutional traders, multi million and billion dollar clients, will seek these Ax's out to buy and sell large quantities of stock. This gives the Ax even more weight, as they are now able to front run a stock in their own account as they buy and sell for their large clients. Combine this with the fact that the Ax uses their client's orders and their own account to trade with a 9:1 margin ratio and you can start to see the power an Ax can have over a stock. An Ax is able to reverse the direction of a stock or stop it cold in its tracks when it looked like a run was inevitable. To do this all the Ax needs to do is sit on the inside quote and not move. For example if AHFS (A High Flying Stock) is trading at 43 x 43 1/8 and GSCO (Goldman Sachs) was showing the inside ask quote of 43 1/8 with a size of 500 then when someone places an order to buy GSCO's 500 shares of AHFS at 43 1/8 GSCO would normally fill the order and leave the inside ask and raise his price. Maybe he would now show 43 3/16 with a new size 500. If GSCO wanted to stop the price of AHFS from rising all he would need to do is keep his quote of 43 1/8 and stay at the ask. Order after order will come in and GSCO would fill the orders and still stay at the same price. This is called "Fading the Trend" and is very difficult to see without a level II screen and Time of Sales Log. This could mean that GSCO has large quantities of stock to sell or is trying to push the stock back down so he can buy even larger quantities than what they are currently selling. When the average trader sees a failed rally they will start to sell their stock and actually help GSCO to push the stock down. The Ax will usually use INCA, Instinet, to purchase the stock on the way down so that the untrained trader will not notice what he is doing. Helping the Ax to accomplish this is the reputation that the Ax carries. Other market makers who also trade AHFS know who the Ax is and what they are capable of doing. So when they see GSCO manipulating a stock in this fashion they too will start to shadow (Copy) the Ax and in doing so help GSCO to lower the price. The smaller the stock the more weight an Ax carries. This does not mean that an Ax is unable to do this in a large stock, only that it takes a bit more time to accomplish their goal.

It is a good idea to get to know the market makers in a stock before you actively trade a stock. Start off by leaving a level II screen up next to the Time of Sales Log and chart on a stock you are interested in trading. If your system allows you highlight the market makers on your level II screen the highlight the top two market makers that you think are acting as the Ax. Update your highlights as necessary until you get the right one. Furthermore, when using your level II screen the Ax will most likely be the last market maker to adjust their price and leave the inside ask or inside bid when the stock runs fast and there is a great deal of buying or selling. You can also visit www.nasdaqtrader.com and type in a stock ticker symbol and see which market maker traded the most volume over a 30 day period. This way whenever you pull up a stock you will instantly be able to locate the Ax and follow what he is doing. You can also pick a stock that has good momentum and a high degree of daily volatility (The difference between the daily high and daily low). Watch the Ax and how he moves. Take note as to what happens on how he trades at the open, close and slow times. What happens when he takes the inside position or widens his spread to the upside? What happens when he is hit on a couple of orders? Does he move or stay? Does he add more to his size or stay the same? Some of the bigger market makers that often act as the Ax in a stock are GSCO, BEST, MLCO, MQNT, HMQT, RSSF, MASH, LEHM, SBSH, FBCO and HRZG.

Once you have the Ax picked out in a stock it is a good idea to shadow him. Watch what he is doing and trade with him. For instance, if the Ax is MLCO and at the open MLCO sits close to or on the inside bid it may look like MLCO is a buyer. Later on if MLCO tightens up his own spread and is close to both the inside bid and inside ask he may now appear to be making a two-sided market and taking money from both the bid and ask spread, never going to far in either direction to tip his hand. As the day goes on however and the Nasdaq starts to turn positive, the futures are trending up and the sector or index the stock trades in is also trending up you may see MLCO continue to sit at or close to the inside bid but now widen his ask price to 7/16 or 1/2 point above the current inside asking price. This is generally a good sign indicating that MLCO has turned bullish on the stock and could be a nice place to enter a long position on the stock. If however the market starts to change and MLCO tightens up his ask price. Don't be afraid to take any profits and exit the position.

Using Instinet is another way the Ax will try to pull money from your account to his. Lets say that a medium sized mutual fund comes up to BEST, Bear Sterns, and wants to purchase 350,000 shares of YMFS, Your Most Favorite Stock. It is currently trading at 31.00 and this mutual fund gives BEST a buy range to work in of 31 to 31 ½. If BEST were to just sit at the inside bid price and try to buy the stock, savvy traders and other market makers would realize what he was doing and jump in front of him or raise the asking price knowing that BEST was a buyer of stock. Soon the price would be above 31 ½ and BEST would need to fill the order from their own inventory. Instead BEST might sit at or close to the inside bid and also trade as INCA on the inside ask with a large size. When other traders see INCA with a size of 10,000 or more on the inside ask it will scare out the weak traders as they quickly post a sell order where BEST will buy them up at the bid price. If some traders do not get the hint as to what BEST is doing and purchase the stock at the asking price from INCA—BEST, Then BEST will continue to stay at the inside ASK with a large size until he forces the stock into capitulation. When this happens BEST will buy back the difference at a lower price from where he shorted it. BEST may even leave the inside bid and trade there as INCA to avoid being detected. A truly great way to trade as long as you have the capital to back it up.

A Head fake, a wiggle and a little bit of dribble. As we discussed earlier an Ax may need to reverse the direction of a stock to gain a greater profit for their own portfolio. One way an Ax does this is with a "Head Fake" scaring or wiggling traders out of their position. If SBSH, Smith Barney, needed to reverse the direction of a stock or force a stock down he could use a basic move that will catch a majority of the traders every time. If SBSH wanted to be a buyer of stock at a lower price than the current quote, and there were not enough sellers to push the stock down, he might sit at the inside bid for a while and slowly increase his spread. Even though he is on the inside bid he may now be more than ½ point above the inside ask. As traders and other market makers see what he, the Ax, is doing they will think he is going bullish on the stock and start to buy. They will then start to increase their asking price thinking that a run is starting to take pace. Some will even start to jump in front of SBSH on the bid. Excitement ensues as traders start buying and the stock starts ticking up. SBSH and or INCA will then quickly jump to the inside ask price with a heavy size of 10,000 shares or more and drop from the bid side of the screen. Traders will see that the Ax is gone from the bid side (no more stability) and now looks to be a seller of stock. This will create a panic. A flood of selling starts and the price drops as everyone tries to sell quickly trying to find a buyer before the stock hits bottom. This usually only takes a few minutes for the setup to take place and if it moves fast enough can even trigger some stop loss orders helping to push the stock down even faster. Once SBSH has pushed the stock down to where he would like to start buying he will use one of the many other tricks he has accumulated to restock his account. This type of market maker trading is usually done during a slow time of the day and not at the open or close.

CHAPTER 13

How to Trade SEC Filings

The Securities and Exchange Commission (SEC) requires all public reporting companies to file documents with this government agency. The documents consist of specific forms, such as the 10-Q. They include standard requests for information that will assist the SEC in regulating a company. Most of these forms are required to be filed electronically, so the public can retrieve them over the Internet. The other forms can be mailed in. The SEC receives and files the electronic documents in a file system called EDGARÔ. The EGDAR documents are available free to the public and can be located at http://www.sec.gov. These documents are informational and are a great resource for shareholders, other companies and potential investors.

The SEC documents include the identity of the major shareholders and all members of the Board of Directors. Also, a descriptive profile of the company is provided annually in the 10-K. You want to know the numbers for the quarterly earnings? Check the 10-Q. These documents can help you put money in your pocket. Investors use these documents to anticipate changes in the stock price. For example, let's take a look at the forms for the proxies: The two most common are: PRE 14A, a Preliminary Proxy Statement (shareholders meeting) and DEF 14A which is the final Proxy Statement (shareholders meeting). The first, a PRE 14A is a notice to all shareholders of an upcoming shareholders meeting. It will cover the place, date, time and proposed items to be discussed at the meeting. The DEF 14A will be the final Proxy statement to come out before the shareholders meeting. This will finalize all items to be addressed at the shareholders meeting including, Election of Board of Directors, a vote on a possible increase in the number of authorized shares of common stock, and any other proposed actions needing shareholders approval.

Edgar files can also be located at other Internet sites and links, including links from many online brokerage firms and stock market research based sites. A site I like offers complimentary information and additional information as a subscription service. It's found at http:www.edgar-online.com. This site is not an official government site, and it is not authorized by the SEC. It is, however, an Edgar service for Internet users. Among other things, this site will alert subscribers to new filings within a minute of its receipt. This service also includes the non-electronically filed documents (regarding the insiders' trading). Copies are made of these paper documents filed at the SEC's office, and then they are scanned into an electronic database for use by the subscribers to their service.

As good as the two mentioned sites are, you may prefer another web site. Searching the Internet under "Edgar" will take you to another web page or two with SEC documents. Searching a topic on the web may be time consuming, but you never know what jewel you will find buried under the heap of electronic information until you take the time to research. Remember to also check for a link to SEC Filings provided by your Internet brokerage firm.

Why do you want to search through all these documents? Well, a public company must disclose much information. It must disclose who owns more than 5% of the company; who the Board members are and how much company stock they own; they must disclose when Board members accumulate company stock and when they sell it; they must disclose the agenda for a shareholders' meeting and when it will be held, and much more.

Each type of requested information is assigned a form number. For example, Form S-8 discloses information regarding stock offered to company employees through a Stock Option Plan or other benefits plan. It will save you a lot of time if you know what you are looking for in each form, because they're packed with wordy legal lingo: Form S-8 filed by Dell Computer Corporation on October 30, 1998, states, "Any statement contained herein or in any document incorporated or deemed to be incorporated by reference herein shall be deemed to be modified or superseded for purposes of this Registration Statement to the extent that a statement contained herein or in any other subsequently filed document which also is or is deemed to be incorporated by reference herein modifies or supersedes such statement." Wow! You want to know what you're looking for.

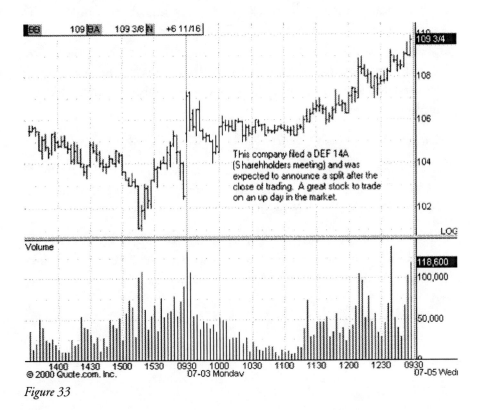

This company filed a DEF 14A (Shareholders meeting) and was expected to announce a split after the close of trading. A great stock to trade on an up day in the market.

Figure 33

The forms you want to be familiar with for short term position trading are Form S-4, Form SC 13D or Form SC 13G and Form DEF 14A:

Form S-4. This form is filed when securities issued in business transactions need to be registered. Notice the CALCULATION OF REGISTRATION FEE below. It is an example of an excerpt of a Form S-4 for Home Depot, Inc. (ticker HD) filed in 1998. This document was filed and the stocks registered upon a merger agreement with Maintenance Warehouse/America Corporation. What you want to pay attention to here is the stock price. If Company A announced plans to purchase stock from Company B at $47 a share and the stock is trading around $32 a share; there is a good chance of the stock price increasing. If the Company B's stock price doesn't increase, then possibly the stock price of Company A will decrease because they may have paid too much for Company B. You can usually get this information from CNBC or market journals, but if you missed the stock details of the merger or acquisition, then this is a good place to check.

XXXXXXXXXXXXXXXXXXXXXXXXXXXXXXXXXXXXXXXXXXXXXXXXXXXXX

APPROXIMATE DATE OF COMMENCEMENT OF PROPOSED SALE TO THE PUBLIC: As soon as practicable following the effectiveness of this Registration Statement.

If any securities being registered on this Form are being offered in connection with the formation of a holding company and there is compliance with General Instruction G, check the following box. f]

CALCULATION OF REGISTRATION FEE

TITLE OF EACH CLASS OF SECURITIES TO BE REGISTERED	AMOUNT TO BE REGISTERED	PROPOSED MAXIMUM OFFERING PRICE PER SHARE (1)	PROPOSED AGGREGATE OFFERING PRICE	MAXIUM AMOUNT OF REGISTRATION FEE(1)
Common Stock, $.05 par valueper share........	5,252,321	$47.00	$246,859,106	$74,806

(1) Estimated solely for the purpose of calculating the registration fee and computed pursuant to Rule 457(f) (2) under the Securities Act of 1933, as amended, based on the aggregate book value of the shares of common stock of Maintenance Warehouse/America Corp. and the partnership interests of certain affiliated limited partnerships to be converted into the right to **receive shares of common stock of The Home Depot, Inc. upon consummation of. the Merger.** The aggregate book value of such shares of common stock and such partnership interests as of October 27, 1996, was $6,468,124.

Form 13D. This form is filed by each person reporting beneficial ownership of company shares of stock, 5% and greater. In pulling up this form for Home Depot, I went as far back as 1994 and still did not locate a form SC 1 3D (this may be common with established public companies). What I did locate was a Form SC 1 3G. This form is completed by specific persons with beneficial ownership of 5% and greater in the company, very similar to the SC 1 3D. The corporation mentioned in the form below has 5.739% interest in the company, totaling 89,789,383 shares. You would like to see Board members with stock ownership, because they make decisions that will impact the price of the stock. And what if a competitor has 5% or more interest in the stock? Could this be the first step to a possible merger or acquisition? Maybe.

XXXXXXXXXXXXXXXXXXXXXXXXXXXXXXXXXXXXXXXXXXXXXXXXXXX

Item 3. This statement is filed pursuant to Rule 13d-1(b) or i3d-2(b) and the person filing, FMR Corp., is a parent holding company in accordance with Section 240.13d-l(b) (ii) (G). (Note: See Item 7).

Item 4. Ownership
(a) Amount Beneficially Owned:

Percent of Class:
(c Number of shares as to which such person has:
(i) Sole power to vote or to direct the vote: 4,467,427
(ii) Shared power to vote or to direct the vote: 0
(iii) Sole power to dispose or to direct the disposition of: 89,789,303
(iv) Shared power to dispose or to direct the disposition of: 0

Item 5. Ownership of Five Percent or Less of a Common Stock. Not applicable.
Item 6. Ownership of More than Five percent on Behalf of Another Person.

Various persons have the right to receive or the power to direct.

XXXXXXXXXXXXXXXXXXXXXXXXXXXXXXXXXXXXXXXXXXXXXXXXXX

Form DEF 14A. This form is the official notice to shareholders of an upcoming annual shareholders' meeting. It is more commonly known as the Proxy Statement. The Proxy Statement notifies the shareholders of the when, where and what of the shareholders' meeting. It includes the date, place to be held and the agenda for the meeting. Shareholders can mail their vote in via Proxy if they are unable to attend the meeting. What we are looking for in the Proxy is if a topic for discussion includes the authorization to increase outstanding shares. See Below. The fourth purpose in the Notice to Shareholders states that they plan to vote to increase the number of authorized shares from 1,000,000,000 to 2,500,000,000. Before a company can announce a stock split they must have enough shares to cover the split—this looks like enough to cover a 2:1 split.

xxxxxxxxxxxxxxxxxxxxxxxxxxxxxxxxxxxxxxxxxxxxxxxxxxxxxxxxxxxxxxxxxxx

THE HOME DEPOT, INC.
2455 PACES FERRY ROAD
ATLANTA, GEORGIA 30339-4024

NOTICE OF ANNUAL MEETING OF STOCKHOLDERS
TO BE HELD MAY 27, 1998

NOTICE is hereby given that the Annual Meeting of Stockholders of The Home Depot, Inc., a Delaware corporation (the "Company" or "Home Depot"), will be held in accordance with its By-laws at the Cobb Galleria Center, 2 Galleria Parkway, Atlanta, Georgia 30339, Wednesday, May 27, 1998, at 10:00 a.m. for the following purposes:

(1) To elect four (4) directors for terms ending with the 2001 Annual Meeting of Stockholders and until their successors are elected and qualified;

(2) To approve an amendment to the Company's Senior Officers' Bonus Pool Plan;

(3) To approve an Executive Officers' Bonus Plan;

(4) To consider and act upon a proposal to amend the Company's Certificate of Incorporation to increase the number of authorized shares of Common Stock from 1,000, 000,000 to 2,500,000, 000; and

(5) To conduct such other business, including consideration of two stockholder proposals, as may properly come before the meeting and any adjournments or postponements of the meeting.

The Common Stock of the Company should be represented as fully as possible at the Annual Meeting. Therefore, it will be appreciated if you will date, sign and return the enclosed proxy at your earliest convenience or vote your shares.

xxxxxxxxxxxxxxxxxxxxxxxxxxxxxxxxxxxxxxxxxxxxxxxxxxxxxxxxxxxxxxx

Check out the other forms, too. They disclose some great stuff. I like some forms that are not required to be filed on the Edgar system, but are required to be filed with the SEC. These forms concern insider trading. They let the SEC and public know when an insider, an officer, director or owner of more than 10% of the company, is intending to sell or buy company stock or has bought or sold stock in the company.

Form 144. This form discloses when insiders are intending to sell their restricted stock. Often this form will be filed by several insiders, say at a 52 week high or when exercising stock options. In looking over this form you want to pay attention to the amount of shares intending to be sold and how many Form 144s are actually filed. If you don't have access to the document, you can look to see how many forms are filed with the SEC. What the trader is learning with this information is the likelihood of a drop in the stock price if there is heavy selling of the stock. When a Form 144 is filed, it doesn't confirm the actual selling of the stock, just the intention to sell. Use this intention to sell in conjunction with an upcoming earnings announcement. The best short sell case scenario would be for some heavy insider selling throughout the quarter with a couple of analyst's downgrades on the stock in the days just before the company announces earnings. Even better would be if the company has a history of negative earnings announcements.

Form 3. This form is filed by every officer, director and owner of more than ten percent of the company to record the buying and selling of company stock. This document will confirm whether the party who filed the Form 144 actually sold stock. It will also disclose if the party purchased stock and the amount of stock purchased. Naturally, if there is heavy selling, we anticipate the stock price to fall, and if there is heavy buying, we anticipate the stock price to rise.

Form 4. This form is to record any changes to the Form 3 after its filing. Note: a Form 3/A is an Amendment to the Form 3; it's for additional information to the Form 3 verses the Form 4 which is for changes to the Form 3.

Form 5. An annual form to be filled out by officers, directors and owners of more than 10% of stock in the company. It discloses the buying and selling of stock.

Use these SEC filings to help direct the anticipated movement of the stock price. The information should confirm what technical indicators are showing you and it will help you to understand the price movement of the stock. For example, if you find a dozen or so Form 144s filed on Intel, and the price drops the next day and continues to drop, you may want to consider selling the stock short—which brings us to our next chapter.

CHAPTER 14

Buy Long, Sell Short, Scalp the Market or Options?

Regardless of what you know today about investing or trading, most of us were taught at an early age everything that there is to know about the stock market, buy low… and sell high. Or is that all there is to know? As I travel around the country teaching classes on the stock market I am always bombarded by the same question, "what looks good?" Now I know they are referring to stocks that I am considering buying, but most of my trading consists of stocks that I have already bought and sold, so as I ponder their question what looks good, I can only come up with the phrase "Buy low and sell high." This thought process is so prevalent in our society that it is often considered the only form of investing. Even licensed professionals will tell you that it is the only consistently true way of making money. As I began my trading career I enlisted the help of a licensed professional and after a few months trading with him I explained that if my results don't change, I'm going to *have* to stop asking you for your help. It was at this time that I began reading every stock market book I could find. And much to my surprise there were many different ways to invest in the stock market. Not only could I buy low and sell high but I could sell high buy low, trade options, scalp the market and even sell low and buy lower. Wow!

BUY LONG. Buy long refers to buying the stock to open up a position. The word long means you own the position. If you buy 100 share of GNCI at $18.00 then you are long 100 shares of GNCI. You will want to buy long when the stock price is moving in an upward direction. Most traders use this strategy more than any other. If you ask them about their recent profits you will hear, "I bought ... at 27 and sold it at 27 ½" or "I bought 500 shares at 16 ¾ and sold it at 17 ½ ". Very rarely do you hear "I sold this option short with a straddle at the out of the money strike on the front month and closed it out by buying back and scalping an 1/8". What most of us know and do is buy long and sell to close (close out your position in the stock.) There are a few things that you must let your broker know when buying into a position, how much to buy, what to buy, at what price to buy and whether or not it is a GTC or Day Order.

Probably the oldest method of buying long is to buy stock after the price has dipped down on its support line (buy low) and is now bouncing upward heading towards the resistance line (sell high).

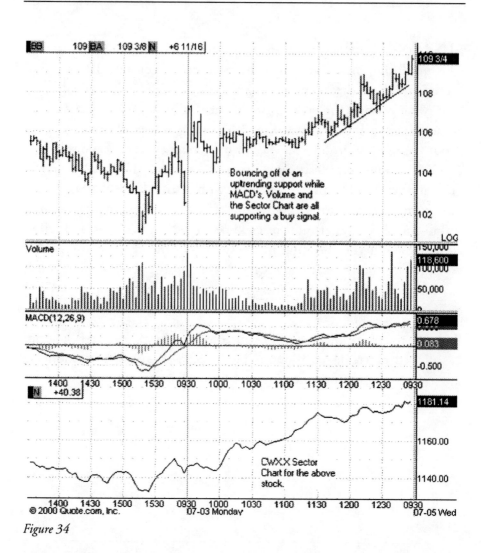

Figure 34

You will be aware of limitations and possibilities if you can detect a support and resistance line. If a stock breaks the high for the day and continues upward, it is a very bullish sign. The price continues to move up even though there is profit taking at the resistance level, which should bring the stock price back down. Also, look at stocks that continue to increase in price even when the market is down. When the stock ignores a bearish market trend, it is a very bullish sign. Buy long on momentum and good news. When the market does turn back up this should be one of the stronger movers for the day.

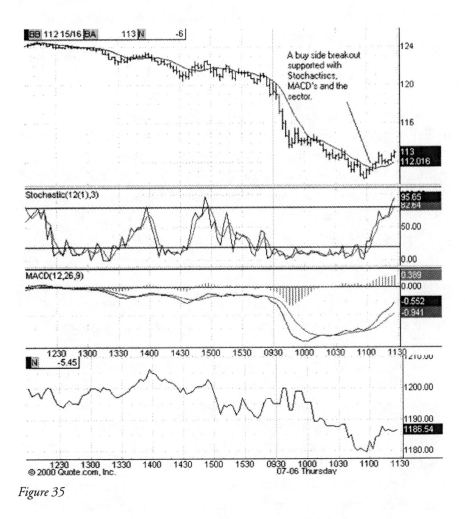

Figure 35

If you find a sector in a bullish trend, you can go long on the big names or if your account will not allow you to purchase some of the high flyers, find an affordable stock trending right along the big name stock in a bullish sector. This will allow you to purchase more shares, thus taking advantage of smaller price movements.

In early March 1999 the Telecommunications Industry, while having some pullbacks, was in an upward trend. On March 3, 1999, QCOM was selling at $75.00 share and another stock in the Telecommunication Industry, SFA, was selling for 32.50 a share. Both are optionable, both were in an upward trending sector, both were trading above 500,000 shares a day and both were in an upward trend. One, however, is half the price of the other and may be a little bit easier to trade (price wise). SFA is the less expensive house in a nice neighborhood. It's something to consider. Aside from price you will also want to check out the difference between the high low spread for the day on each. If QCOM is a $75.00 dollar stock and has an average difference of $6.00 between its high and low price and SFA has only a $1.50 difference then trading 433 shares of QCOM might be a better trading opportunity than 1000 share of SFA.

SELL SHORT. Short selling can only be done on an up tick. An up tick is an increase in the price of the stock. The market makers must be moving the price upward. You sell the stock at its high, wait for it to drop, buy it back at its low, and you keep the difference, minus commissions. Many traders have never tried to short sell a stock and by eliminating this from their trading style they are also eliminating ½ of their trading opportunities. We have always been told that to make money in the stock market we must buy low and sell high. Although this is true, it is not always correct. We can also sell high and *then* buy low. Even if you are an experienced trader, the first time you sell a stock short and then buy it back to close, you will probably feel a bit giddy. But with time it will become second nature and whether you buy long or sell short you will be more comfortable in any market while increasing your trading opportunities. Without short selling in your arsenal you will be doomed to look for stocks to go long on, on days or months when the market is telling you to sell. You have probably heard the phrase "The trend is your friend," don't try to fight it.

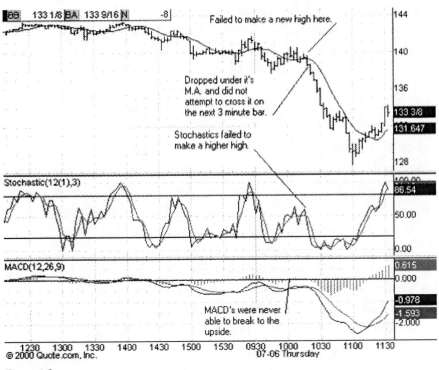

Figure 36

One approach for finding a stock to short is to try looking for the worst stock in the best sector. This stock will automatically be getting a boost from the sector. It's sort of like buying the worst house in a nice neighborhood. It automatically makes your house worth more. If the stock is under performing now, you can wait for a down turn in the sector and then short the stock to buy back later at a lower price.

Selling a stock short can only be done in a margin/short account. The language used to place this trade would be, *"I would like to sell short 500 shares of CPQ at a limit of 25 13/16 for the day."* The downside to this strategy, of course, is if the stock price goes up you may have to buy it at a higher price. Ouch!

SCALP THE MARKET. To scalp the market is to make money when the stock price rolls sideways. You skim an 1/8 or 1/16 of a point or whatever you can get. You do this repetitively throughout the day with large quantities of stock. Trading stock works better for this strategy than trading options, since the price movement is so slight you want a tick for tick movement. Scalping the market usually takes some big cash because to profit from a teeny (1/16) you need quantity. I have an account that if I trade1000 shares or more, the commission fees don't exist. So, I don't have to worry about breaking even after commission fees when playing this strategy. If you can buy 1000 shares and take an 1/8 of a point without commissions, that's $120. If you do this several more times throughout the day, you could make $500 or so a day. You can take a little pop in the stock and get out. Some brokerage firms won't charge you commission fees after the first trade if you buy and sell the same stock the same day. If you like this strategy, then read the fine print in your brokerage contract or check with your broker about the commission fees. This strategy can keep you busy during the slower periods of the market, following the first hour until the last ½ hour. The lunchtime hours can be especially non-eventful.

Some traders only trade this strategy, others may entertain themselves with it during the off peak hours. The key to scalping is to determine the overall trend of the market first and then the overall trend of the stock and the sector it trades in. If the overall trend of the market is sideways but slightly up then scalp only stocks that are in an uptrend from a bullish sector. But when entering into this scalping play enter into it with a buy first. Do not short it to open the position. Since the stock is in an uptrend it has a better chance of rising than falling. If you short it first then you might have to buy it back at a higher price. If the overall trend of the market for the day is sideways but slightly down then you might want to look for a stock in a downtrend from a weak sector. When entering into this type of scalping play you will want to short it first. Do not buy it to open the position. Since the overall trend of the stock and sector is down it has a better chance of dropping then it does of going up and you don't want to have to sell it at a lower price for a loss.

OPTIONS. If given the chance to position trade stocks or options, I'll choose stocks the majority of the time. The reasoning behind this is so that I will not have to pay any time value and thus giving me a tick for tick movement in profit with the stock movement. However there are those who prefer to trade options to stock. Their reasoning is usually a lack of funds to purchase sufficient quantities of stock. Buying options gives you the ability to buy 10 contracts (1000 shares) at a substantial discount to buying 1000 shares of a stock. Option traders buy and sell calls and puts, depending on the direction of the market. Because of the lack of a tick for tick movement like you receive with stock, you may want to look for a price movement of a point or so. Option trading is becoming more and more popular. There are now 5 different exchanges to trade options with. This increased competition between market makers is benefiting the average trader as option spreads are becoming tighter and tighter allowing many more trading opportunities.

MMID	Bid	Size	Time		MMID	Ask	Size	Time
INCA	50 3/16	2,900-	11:48:26		ISLD	50 1/4	2,700+	11:48:30
PRUS	50 3/16	100-	11:48:17		DLJP	50 1/4	1,000+	11:48:13
SBSH	50 3/16+	100-	11:48:03		HRZG	50 1/4	100-	11:48:25
NITE	50 3/16+	100	11:47:54		JPMS	50 1/4	100-	11:48:22
GSCO	50 1/8+	1,000	11:48:00		GSCO	50 3/8+	1,000	11:48:00
BEST	50 1/8+	1,000	11:47:43		INCA	50 3/8+	600+	11:47:01
MASH	50 1/8+	1,000	11:47:27		REDI	50 3/8-	100-	11:48:12
ISLD	50 1/8-	900-	11:48:31		FBCO	50 3/8+	100-	11:47:00
ARCA	50 1/8+	500-	11:47:25		MASH	50 3/8	100	11:43:22
DLJP	50 1/8+	100	11:47:43		CANT	50 3/8	100	10:19:40
SELZ	50 1/8+	100	11:47:38		ARCA	50 7/16	500	11:44:14
FBCO	49 7/8+	100	11:47:00		MWSE	50 7/16		

You can buy the stock for 50 3/16.

MMID	Bid	Size	Time		MMID	Ask	Size	Time
amex	3 3/4	1	01/01 00:		pacx	3 7/8	1	01/01 00:
cboe	3 3/4	1	01/01 00:		cboe	4	1	01/01 00:
pacx	3 1/2	1	01/01 00:		amex	4 1/8		

Or you can buy the 50 call and pay time.

© 2000 Quote.com, Inc.

Figure 37

To understand the true difference between trading stocks vs. options you must understand the breakdown of an option. Options are made up of two parts, intrinsic and extrinsic value. In simple terms, the intrinsic value is the amount paid to the seller so they break even when they sell you an option and the extrinsic value is the amount paid to the seller for holding the option for a specified period of time. Also known as time value. You may want to know the Delta on your option, so you know how much the price needs to move before you get what you want from your option. Deep In-the-money options work best for short term trading. Lets look at a quote of WCOM. Figure 36

43 3/8 x 43 7/16 volume of 28,355,824

April calls

April 32 1/2 calls: 11 1/16 x 11 1/4, Intrinsic value of 10.94 and Extrinsic value of .31

April 35 calls: 9 1/2 x 9 5/8, Intrinsic value of 8.44 and Extrinsic value of 1.18

April 37 ½ calls: 7 1/4 x 7 3/8, Intrinsic value of 5.94 and Extrinsic value of 1.44

April 40 calls: 5 1/8 x 5 1/4, Intrinsic value of 4.44 and Extrinsic value of .81

April 42 ½ calls: 3 3/16 x 3 1/4, Intrinsic value of 1.94 and Extrinsic value of 1.31

April 45 calls: 1 15/16 x 2, Intrinsic value of 0 and Extrinsic value of 2.00

To find the intrinsic value of an option: (stock price—option strike price)
Using WCOM and the April 32 1/2 calls (43.44—32.50 = 10.94)
To find the extrinsic value of an option: (option price—intrinsic value)
Using WCOM and the April 32 1/2 calls (11.25—10.94 = .31)

If you were to buy WCOM stock at 43.44 and it moved up to 43.75 you would be able to sell the stock for a .31cent profit, a tick for tick movement. Had you bought the April 32 1/2 call for 11 1/4 when the stock was at 43.44 and then the stock moved up to 43.75 the option might not have moved at all. Remember that you were paying .31 cents for time value and until the stock moves *more* than .31 cents the market may not change his option price. As long as you are paying time value the market maker has the ability to play with the option price, especially if he sees you have an order on the floor for a buy or sell. After studying a few options trades you can see why it can be more profitable to trade stocks over options. However options provide a low cost alternative to trading stock, especially higher priced stocks. And options trading can limit your downside, as your monetary risk for an $11.25 option is less than a $43.44 stock.

For a more detailed quote on options pricing, check with your broker, technical analysis software or an Internet site, such as www.amex.com or www.cboe.com for a Delta or theoretical pricing. Practice trading on paper to help determine your comfort level and expectations. Study calls and puts and learns how to roll out of them if you have to. Practice trades with larger quantities of lower priced stock and with higher priced stock with greater price fluctuations.

If you buy an out of the money option and expect to get your profit in only a few days, you are really betting on your luck. When I go long to trade options and I expect the stock price to go up, I buy an in the money call with as little time as possible or I sell an out of the money put with as little time as possible. If I expect the stock price to go down, I buy an in the money put with as little time as possible or I sell an out of the money call with as little time as possible. I started out position trading only with options and then switched to stock for the tick for tick movement in the price. I also wanted to avoid paying for any time premium. Trading this way allowed for quicker profits but a lower rate of return.

Trading options was a great place for me to start and I continue to trade option strategies today, but for different reasons than before.

POSITION TRADING WITH OPTIONS

"I think the stock price is going to go up. What could I do?"

Buy an in the money call with as little time as possible.

Sell an out of the money put with as little time as possible. This means selling the current month at a strike price above the current stock price.

"I think the stock price is going to go down. What could I do?"

Buy an in the money put with as little time as possible.

Sell an out of the money call with as little time as possible.

A profitable trader will learn to harness all styles of trading; long, short, scalping and options. The most basic of rules to remember is not to try and fight the market. On days when the market is trading up, stick to buying stocks in an uptrend in a bullish sector. On days when the market is down, stick to shorting stocks in a downtrend in a weak sector. On days when the market is going sideways try scalping the stock. When scalping a stock that is in an uptrend go long on the stock first and when scalping a stock that is in a downtrend, short the stock to open the position and buy to close. For example, if DELL were trading in an uptrend for the last 45 days I would not want to short the stock. On days when the market is trending sideways and I wanted to play DELL I would start by going long on DELL and then sell to close the position. If I were to start the trade by going short there is a good chance that DELL could rise higher because it's overall trend was to the upside.

CHAPTER 15

The Bell Rings

I once watched a movie called Apocalypse Now where Robert Duvall, an aggressive marine officer stood in the middle of a burning battle field with charred cinders and death all around and declared "I love the smell of Napalm in the morning." In a way this scenario best describes what it is like to trade amateur hour in the stock market. Amateur hour is referred to as the first trading hour of the day. It is called this because seasoned investors generally trade into the market the last 1/2 hour of trading. It is the investor that works 8-5 or 9-6 who, after studying each night analyzing charts, news and fundamentals, will call up their broker first thing in the morning and place an order. They buy into a position then head off to work completely unaware of market makers who typically inflate a stocks price at the open only to bring it right back down in a matter of minutes. How often have you seen the DOW open up 50 points and then pull back to -40 points and end up + 60 points all within the first hour of the trading day. As a short term trader I look for one thing in a stock, volatility! I want the stocks to do something. I don't care what as long as it just does not go sideways. I don't have a preference for whether a stock trades up or down. I let the market and stock tell me which way to trade.

Before we get to far into this chapter I want to mention a couple of rules about trading the opening hour of the market. #1 and most important, *never place a market order!* Market makers know that any market order placed in the first hour of the day is from a novice investor and should be treated so. Market makers make their money buy buying low and selling high, selling high and then buying low and by gaining the spread of a stock. So if they think they can sell a novice investor a stock for 26 1/8 when the inside quote was 25 7/8 buy 26, then they probably will. Now you might be saying that paying only 1/8 extra is not a lot, and it isn't if you are an investor. However as a position trader it can be half of what you wanted to make on a trade. Also remember that the market maker could have filled you at 26 1/2. When you placed your order at market you were telling the person receiving the order that **you don't care what price you get filled at as long as you get filled.** Instead of a market order try using a limit order. If the stock is running away from you then try your limit order 1/8 to 3/16 of a point away from the price. An example would be a stock in a volatile sector such as the Internet or Computer sector. Maybe your looking at one of the most active stocks and it is ticking up in price every 15 seconds or so. If your brokerage firm takes an average of 10 to 15 seconds to get your trade to the market you might place a limit order to buy your stock 1/8 point above the current asking price. This way you will have a better shot at getting filled. In most cases if the stock has not yet ticked up there is still a strong chance that you will be filled at the current ask price. What you are doing is eliminating the extra profit a market maker will make on your account with a market order and setting a reachable limit price for your fill.

If you think you are ready to handle amateur hour and start making some money then it is now time for your trading game plan.

1) **Night Time Prep Work.** It is a good idea to purchase charting software. The one that I use is TC2000. You will be amazed at the stocks you will be able to find when writing scans that fit your style of trading. *See Chapter 16 for scan criteria.* Each night you will want to scan for stocks that you can use as possible trading candidates for the next trading day. Perhaps these will be stocks that gapped open and closed at the high or a trending stock with a great deal of volatility in a price

range that you can afford. After awhile you will get to know a lot of these stocks as they continue to pop up on your scans. When there are times, and there are, when it appears that there are no stocks to trade, you can go to your favorites list and scalp 1/2 of a point from the market.

Listen to aftermarket announcements on CNBC or through a website such as http://investor.cnet.com or www.briefing.com. Here you will learn of anything that might potentially move the market the next morning. This will let you concentrate your research more towards the stocks that will benefit from the markets moves.

Prepare your list of potential slam candidates. Some for an upside bounce and some for a continued downside fall.

Look for impending earnings runs.

Look for tomorrows Economic Numbers. If Retail sales numbers are to be released tomorrow at 8:30 AM Eastern then have a list of retail stocks that are trending up with a possible earnings announcement in the next couple of weeks. It would not hurt for the stock to have been upgraded and also have a history of consecutive positive earnings announcements. A strong Economic Retail number will help investors to feel more comfortable about buying in the sector or even push more investors to the sector. Market makers will also know this and start to artificially inflate the retail stocks. You can also prepare a list of retail stocks that are trending down, ones that could fall even further if the Economic Retail numbers come out poorly.

If it was a down day in the market, look for any stocks that had some positive news such as a split announcement, a positive earnings announcement or an upgrade or two. If the market and or sector that the stock trades in had a bad day it will bring down the stocks that trade along with it. Tomorrow will be a new day providing a chance for the stock to recoup its losses. Traders will feel more comfortable going long on a stock with good news on days when the market is also doing well. To see how this works just imagine if you were to add an addition to your home making it more valuable. Just as you completed it you found out that the state was putting a freeway right through your neighborhood and 20 feet from your backyard. It does not matter how much work (good news) you added to your house. Your houses value will drop because the neighborhood your house is in is now worth less money.

Another one I like to do is to check out www.cnbc.com and see which CEO's will be featured for the upcoming day. It will even tell you which hour of the day they will be on giving you plenty of time to research the company. Usually CNBC will only put on a CEO if there is something special happening with the company i.e. stock split, earnings, large movement in stock price, new technology… If the CEO comes out on CNBC, is very upbeat, professional and touts their stock it could give the stock an immediate boost. Also if the CNBC commentator says anything positive on the stock while the CEO is on the air it can be a double push. It is not uncommon for a stock to climb 1 point or more in the 3 minutes that the CEO is on the air.

All of this may sound like it is time consuming and too much work but it is preparation that makes a good trader. Without creating a list of stocks with which to trade from in both an up and down market you will be left to make rash decisions on stocks that are trading when you know little about them. Suppose that you looked at the most actively traded stocks and found one that was down 2 1/8 for the day on a day that the market in which it trades in was also down. You pull up a 3 minute chart and see that it is trending down and trending below its 5 minute moving average. Stochastics and MACD's are also showing a downtrend. In a rush you decide to short the stock only to find it flatten out and then reverse direction and head back up. Had you done some further research and not made a rash trade you might have seen that the stock has a good daily long term support at the price you shorted it, had a daily spread (the high minus the low) of 2.00 which it had already reached when you got in, was in a strong sector, and was coming up on earnings in 6 days. As in any cash venture, preparation should be consideration #1.

2) **AM Prep Work.** You went to bed feeling good about the list you came up with to trade. However things can and will change overnight so it is a good idea to double check you list and see if any new news is out on your stocks. Suppose one of your slam candidates has had a downgrade or an earnings candidate has had another upgrade during the night. Reorganize your list to meet the open.

   Checkout the overseas trading. Many of our larger stocks also trade overseas and could have finished the session up. Also if the Japanese and European markets had strong closes it will transfer over to our market. Check out www.cnbc.com for overseas market numbers.

   Use your real time software to see which stocks are trading heavy in premarket trading and where the market leaders are trading. It is safe to say that if MSFT, INTC, CSCO, DELL, YHOO, and ORCL are all trading up in premarket trading then the Nasdaq should have some positive momentum at the open. What if you find a stock that is not normally on the premarket heavy volume list? Spend some time and research it. Why is it moving? Are there any other stocks that will get a sympathy movement from it? What are its daily spreads, support and resistance lines…?

   Which Economic indicators have already come out? Do you need to revise your list again? Maybe they were flat and now you wont trade any stocks from you retail list.

   What is CNBC saying about the upcoming trading day? Are they parading around analysts who are bullish or bearish? When they cut to the NYSE trading floor what are the comments coming from there? Are they talking about any market moving news that could affect the stocks on your list?

Where are the S&P Futures and the Nasdaq Futures? Both can be found on the bottom right hand corner on CNBC prior to the opening bell. S&P Futures + 8.00 or more or –8.00 or more and Nasdaq Futures +45.00 or more or –45.00 or more will indicate strong opens to the up or downside depending on whether or not the number was positive or negative.

How about the 30 year bond yield? Is it up or down? If it is trading up then there can be a negative pull on the market and if trading down then there can be some positive pressure for stocks.

3) **The Open.** You are now set for the opening bell. We have taken you from a telephone line to a computer, from setting up an account to trading in a dummy account, from research to technicals, from trading strategies to reading the open. You now have what I use on a daily basis to make a living in the market. You will find that you will grow to like some of the strategies I have shown you and maybe even toss out some of the others. Only you know which ones fit your needs.

The Bell has rung, what will you do?

About the Author

Michael D. Coval is a professional speaker and trader who has taught thousands of students his secrets of success in the stock market. He speaks on trading topics and the advanced uses of options. His classes are designed for traders who wish to generate a livable income. He is a featured trader on Writingputs.com where he shares some of his real trades and his reasoning behind each one, and a financial editor for IncomeTrader.com. He markets a series of educational material for the active trader. Along with his wife Catherine and son Alex he makes his home in Washington State where he originally attended college for Chemical Engineering. He can be contacted at Questions@writingputs.com

Appendix

NDX.X NASDAQ-100 Index (CBOE)

AAPL Apple Computer, Inc.	BGEN Biogen, Inc.
ADBE Adobe Systems Incorporated	BMCS BMC Software, Inc.
ADCT ADC Telecommunications, Inc.	BMET Biomet, Inc.
	CATP Cambridge Tech Partners, Inc.
ADPT Adaptec, Inc.	CBRL CBRL Group Inc.
ADSK Autodesk, Inc.	CEFT Concord EFS, Inc.
ALTR Altera Corporation	CEXP Corporate Express
AMAT Applied Materials, Inc.	CHIR Chiron Corporation
AMGN Amgen Inc.	CIEN CIENA Corporation
AMZN Amazon.com, Inc.	CMCSK Comcast Corporation
ANDW Andrew Corporation	CMGI CMGI, Inc.
APCC American Power Conversion Corp.	CMVT Comverse Technology, Inc.
APOL Apollo Group, Inc.	CNET CNET Networks, Inc.
ATHM At Home Corporation	CNTO Centocor Inc
ATML Atmel Corporation	CNXT Conexant Systems, Inc.
BBBY Bed Bath & Beyond Inc.	COMR Comair Holdings, Inc.

COMS 3Com Corporation	LCOS Lycos, Inc. LLTC Linear Technology Corporation
COST Costco Wholesale Corporation	LNCR Lincare Holdings Inc.
CPWR Compuware Corporation	LVLT Level 3 Communications, Inc.
CSCO Cisco Systems, Inc.	MCHP Microchip Technology Incorporated
CTAS Cintas Corporation	
CTXS Citrix Systems, Inc.	MCLD McLeodUSA Incorporated
DELL Dell Computer Corporation	MLHR Herman Miller, Inc.
DLTR Dollar Tree Stores, Inc.	MOLX Molex Incorporated
EFII Electronics for Imaging, Inc.	MSFT Microsoft Corporation
	MUEI Micron Electronics, Inc.
ERICY LM Ericsson Telephone Company	MXIM Maxim Integrated Products, Inc.
ERTS Electronic Arts Inc.	NETA Network Associates, Inc.
FAST Fastenal Company	
FHCC First Health Group Corp.	NOVL Novell, Inc.
FISV Fiserv, Inc.	NTLI NTL Incorporated
GBLX Global Crossing Ltd	NWAC Northwest Airlines Corporation
GENZ Genzyme General	NXTL Nextel Communications, Inc.
IMNX Immunex Corporation	
INTC Intel Corporation	ORCL Oracle Corporation
INTU Intuit Inc.	PAYX Paychex, Inc.
JDSU JDS Uniphase Corporation	PCAR PACCAR Inc
KLAC KLA-Tencor Corporation	PHSY PacifiCare Health Systems, Inc.

PMTC Parametric Technology Corporation	SSCC Smurfit-Stone Container Corp.
PSFT PeopleSoft, Inc.	STEI Stewart Enterprises, Inc.
QCOM QUALCOMM Incorporated	
QTRN Quintiles Transnational Corp.	SUNW Sun Microsystems, Inc.
	TECD Tech Data Corporation
QWST Qwest Communications Int Inc.	TLAB Tellabs, Inc.
	USAI USA Networks, Inc.
ROST Ross Stores, Inc.	VISX VISX, Incorporated
RTRSY Reuters Group PLC	VRTS VERITAS Software Corporation
RXSD Rexall Sundown, Inc.	
SANM Sanmina Corporation	VTSS Vitesse Semiconductor Corporation
SBUX Starbucks Corporation	WCOM WorldCom, Inc.
SEBL Siebel Systems, Inc.	WTHG Worthington Industries, Inc.
SIAL Sigma-Aldrich Corporation	XLNX Xilinx, Inc.
SNPS Synopsys, Inc.	YHOO Yahoo! Inc.
SPLS Staples, Inc.	
SPOT PanAmSat Corporation	

Index Options

HKO.X Hong Kong Option Index (AMEX)	XCI.X Computer Technology Index (AMEX)
XAL.X Airline Index (AMEX)	EUR.X EUROTOP 100 Index (AMEX)
PLN.X Airline Sector Index (PHLX)	FPP.X Forest & Paper Products Sector Index (PHLX)
BKX.X KBW Bank Sector Index (PHLX)	XAU.X Gold and Silver Sector Index (PHLX)
BTK.X Biotechnology Index (AMEX)	GTC.X GSTI Composite Index (CBOE)
XBD.X Securities Broker/Dealer Index (The) (AMEX)	GHA.X GSTI Hardware Index (CBOE)
AUX.X Automotive Index (CBOE)	GIN.X GSTI Internet Index (CBOE)
CWX.X Computer Software Index (CBOE)	GIP.X GSTI Multimedia Networking Index (CBOE)
EVX.X Environmental Index (CBOE)	GSM.X GSTI Semiconductor Index (CBOE)
GAX.X Gaming Index (CBOE)	GSV.X GSTI Services Index (CBOE)
INX.X CBOE Internet Index (CBOE)	GSO.X GSTI Software Index (CBOE)
MEX.X Mexico Index (CBOE)	
TXX.X Technology Index (CBOE)	
NYA.X NYSE Composite Index (CBOE)	PSE.X PSE Technology 100 Index (PACX)

DJX.X Dow Jones Industrial Average (CBOE)	LTX.X Latin 15 Index (CBOE)
	XMI.X Major Market Index (AMEX)
DTX.X Dow Jones Transportation Average (CBOE)	MXY.X Mexico Index (The) (AMEX)
DUX.X Dow Jones Utility Average (CBOE)	CMR.X Morgan Stanley Consumer Index (AMEX)
GOX.X Gold Index (CBOE)	CYC.X Morgan Stanley Cyclical Index (AMEX)
HUI.X Gold BUGS Index (AMEX)	
ISX.X INDEX:ISX.X	HMO.X Morgan Stanley Healthcare Payor Index (AMEX)
LGO.X Lipper/Salomon Growth Funds Index (CBOE)	RXP.X Morgan Stanley Healthcare Product Index (AMEX)
LIO.X Lipper/Salomon Growth & Income Funds Index (CBOE)	RXH.X Morgan Stanley Healthcare Provider (AMEX)
MXX.X Indice de Precios y Cotizaciones (IPC) Index (CBOE)	MSH.X Morgan Stanley High-Technology 35 Index (AMEX)
NFT.X Morgan Stanley Multinational Company Index (CBOE)	XTC.X North American Telecommunications Index (AMEX)
NWX.X Networking Index (The) (AMEX)	NDX.X NASDAQ-100 Index (CBOE)
OIX.X Oil Index (CBOE)	
XII.X Institutional Index (AMEX)	XOC.X National Over-The-Counter Sector Index
IIX.X AMEX Internet Index (AMEX)	XNG.X Natural Gas Index (The) (AMEX)
JPN.X Japan Index (AMEX)	

NIK.X Nikkei 300 Index (CBOE)	HCX.X S&P Health Care Index (CBOE)
XOI.X Oil Index (AMEX)	IUX.X S&P Insurance Index (CBOE)
DRG.X Pharmaceutical Index (AMEX)	MID.X S&P 400 MidCap Index (AMEX)
PNX.X Phone Sector Index (PHLX)	RLX.X S&P Retail Index (CBOE)
RIX.X REIT Index (CBOE)	SML.X S&P SmallCap 600 Index (CBOE)
RUT.X Russell 2000 Index (CBOE)	TRX.X S&P Transportation Index (CBOE)
OEX S&P 100 Index (CME)	SOX.X Semiconductor Sector Index (PHLX)
SPX.X S&P 500 Index (CBOE)	HFX.X SuperCap Sector Index (PHLX)
SPL.X S&P 500 Index—Long-Term (CBOE)	TPX.X U.S. Top 100 Index (PHLX)
BIX.X S&P Banks Index (CBOE)	UTY.X Utility Sector Index (PHLX)
SGX.X S&P 500/BARRA Growth Index (CBOE)	VLE.X Value Line Composite Index (PHLX)
SVX.X S&P 500/BARRA Value Index (CBOE)	WSX.X Wilshire Small Cap Index (PACX)
CEX.X S&P Chemical Index (CBOE)	

NASDAQ 100 FINANCIALS

SRCE 1st Source Corporation	CBCF Citizens Banking Corporation
ADVNA ADVANTA Corp.	CBSH Commerce Bancshares, Inc.
ALFA Alfa Corporation	CFBX Community First Bankshares, Inc.
ALLC Allied Capital Corporation	
AMFI Amcore Financial, Inc.	CBSS Compass Bancshares, Inc.
ANAT American National Insurance Company	CORS CORUS Bankshares, Inc.
	DBCC Data Broadcasting Corporation
AMTD AmeriTrade Holding Corporation	
	DORL Doral Financial Corporation
AMMB AMRESCO, Inc.	EGRP E*TRADE Group, Inc.
AGII Argonaut Group, Inc.	ERIE Erie Indemnity Company
ASBC Associated Banc-Corp	FBAN F.N.B. Corporation
ASFC Astoria Financial Corporation	FITB Fifth Third Bancorp
BNKU Bank United Corporation	FACO First Alliance Corporation
BKNG Banknorth Group, Inc.	FCNCA First Citizens BancShares, Inc.
BOKF BOK Financial Corporation	
CFFN Capitol Federal Financial	FFBC First Financial Bancorp.
CAFC Carolina First Corporation	FMBI First Midwest Bancorp, Inc.
COFI Charter One Financial, Inc.	FSCO First Security Corporation
CINF Cincinnati Financial Corporation	FMER FirstMerit Corporation
	FULT Fulton Financial Corporation

HBHC Hancock Holding Company	NWSB Northwest Bancorp, Inc.
HGIC Harleysville Group Inc.	OCAS Ohio Casualty Corporation
HARS Harris Financial, Inc.	OLDB Old National Bancorp
HBAN Huntington Bancshares Incorporated	SABB Pacific Capital Bancorp
ICII Imperial Credit Industries, Inc.	PBCT People's Bank
ICBC Independence Community Bank Corp.	PHBK Peoples Heritage Financial Group, Inc.
IBOC International Bancshares Corporation	BPOP Popular, Inc.
	PLFE Presidential Life Corporation
IRWN Irwin Financial Corporation	PREN Price Enterprises, Inc.
KSTN Keystone Financial, Inc.	PBKS Provident Bankshares Corporation
NITE Knight Trading Group, Inc.	PFGI Provident Financial Group, Inc.
MAFB MAF Bancorp, Inc.	
MRIS Marshall & Ilsley	QCSB Queens County Bancorp, Inc.
MRBK Mercantile Bankshares Corporation	RGBK Regions Financial Corporation
NBAK National Bancorp of Alaska, Inc. NCBC National Commerce Bancorporation	RCBK Richmond County Financial Corp.
NTBK Net.B@nk, Inc.	RIGS Riggs National Corporation
NXCD NextCard, Inc.	RSLN Roslyn Bancorp, Inc.
NTRS Northern Trust Corporation	STBA S&T Bancorp, Inc.

SAFC SAFECO Corporation	TRMK Trustmark Corporation
SEIC SEI Investments Company	UMBF UMB Financial Corporation
SIGI Selective Insurance Group, Inc.	
SIVB Silicon Valley Bancshares	UBSI United Bankshares, Inc.
SKYF Sky Financial Group, Inc.	UNIT Unitrin, Inc.
SOTR SouthTrust Corporation	USTB UST Corp.
SVRN Sovereign Bancorp, Inc.	BKLY W. R. Berkley Corporation
SPBC St. Paul Bancorp	WFSL Washington Federal, Inc.
STFC State Auto Financial Corporation	WBST Webster Financial Corporation
SUSQ Susquehanna Bancshares, Inc.	WSBC WesBanco, Inc.
TROW T. Rowe Price Associates, Inc.	WABC Westamerica Bancorporation
TBFC Telebanc Financial Corporation	WEBC Western Bancorp
PIOG Pioneer Group, Inc. (The)	WBPR W Holding Company Incorporated
TREN Trenwick Group	WTNY Whitney Holding Corporation
TRST TrustCo Bank Corp NY	ZION Zions Bancorporation

S&P 100

OEX S&P 100 Index (CME)	BCC Boise Cascade Corp
OEX.X S&P 100 Index (CBOE)	BMY Bristol Myers Squibb Co
AA Alcoa Inc.	BC Brunswick Corp
ALT Allegheny Teledyne	BNI Burlington Northn Santa Fe
AXP American Express Co	CBS CBS Corp
AEP American Elec Pwr Inc	CI Cigna Corp
AIG American Intl Group Inc	CPB Campbell Soup Co
AIT Ameritech Corporation	CEN Ceridian Corporation
AGC American Gen Corp	CHA Champion Intl Corp
T AT&T Corp	CSCO Cisco Systems, Inc.
ARC Atlantic Richfield Company	C Citigroup Inc
AVP Avon Prods Inc	CGP Coastal Corp
BHI Baker Hughes Inc	KO Coca Cola Co
BAC Bank Amer Corp	CL Colgate Palmolive Co
ONE Bank One Corp	COL Columbia / Hca Healthcare Co
BAX Baxter Intl Inc	
BEL Bell Atlantic Corp	CSC Computer Sciences Corp
BS Bethlehem Steel	DAL Delta Air Lines Inc Del
BDK Black & Decker Corp	DIS The Walt Disney Company
BA Boeing Co	DOW DOW Chem Co

DD Du Pont E I De Nemours & Co	IP International Paper Co
EK Eastman Kodak Co	JNJ Johnson & Johnson
ETR Entergy Corp New	KM K Mart Corp
XON Exxon Corp	LTD Limited Inc
FDX FedEx Corporation	LU Lucent Technologies Inc
FLR Fluor Corp	MKG Mallinckrodt Inc.
F Ford Mtr Co Del	MAY MAY Dept Stores Co
GD General Dynamics Corp	MCD Mcdonalds Corp
GE General Electric Co.	MRK Merck & Co Inc
GM General Motors Corp.	MER Merrill Lynch & Co Inc
HAL Halliburton Co	MSFT Microsoft Corporation
HET Harrahs Entmt Inc HRS Harris Corp Del	MMM Minnesota Mng & Mfg Co
HIG Hartford Finl Svcs Group Inc	MOB Mobil Corp
HNZ Heinz H J Co	MTC Monsanto Co
HWP Hewlett Packard Co	NSM National Semiconductor Corp
HM Homestake Mng Co	NSC Norfolk Southn Corp
HON Honeywell International	NT Nortel Networks Corp.
INTC Intel Corporation	OXY Occidental Pete Corp
IBM International Business Machines Corp	ORCL Oracle Corporation
IFF International Flavrs & Fragr	PEP Pepsico Inc
	PNU Pharmacia & Upjohn Inc

PRD Polaroid Corporation	TOY Toys R Us Inc
PG Procter & Gamble Co	USB US Bancorp Del
RAL Ralston-purina Lg-t	UCM Unicom Corp
RTN.B Raytheon Co	UIS Unisys Corporation
ROK Rockwell Intl Corp New	UTX United Technologies Corp
SLB Schlumberger Limited	WMT Wall Mart Stores Inc
S Sears Roebuck & Co	WFC Wells Fargo & Co New
SO Southern Company	WY Weyerhaeuser Co
TAN Tandy Corp	WMB Williams Cos Inc
TEK Tektronix Inc	XRX Xerox Corp
TXN Texas Instrs Inc	

All Index Symbols

ADR.X International Market Index	CWX.X Computer Software Index (CBOE)
AUX.X Automotive Index (CBOE)	CYC.X Morgan Stanley Cyclical Index (AMEX)
BANKX NASDAQ Banking Index	
BGX.X Biotech Index	CYO.X CYC.X Settlement Valuation
BIX.X S&P Banks Index (CBOE)	DGL.X DRG.X LEAPS Index
BKL.X BTK LEAPS Index	DGO.X $DRG.X LEAPS Settlement Valuation
BKX.X KBW Bank Sector Index (PHLX)	DRG.X Pharmaceutical Index (AMEX)
BTK.X Biotechnology Index (AMEX)	DRO.X $DRG.X Settlement Valuation
BTS.X BTK.X Settlement Valuation	
CEX.X S&P Chemical Index (CBOE)	ERI.X FT-Actuary Index Value in $
CMR.X Morgan Stanley Consumer Index (AMEX)	EUR.X EUROTOP 100 Index (AMEX)
COMP Dow Jones Composite Average (sm)	EUV.X $EUR.X Settlement Valuation
COMPX NASDAQ Composite Index	EVS.X CBOE Environmental Index Settlement
CSO.X CMR.X Settlement Valuation	EVX.X Environmental Index (CBOE)
CWS.X CBOE Computer Software Index Settlement	FPP.X Forest & Paper Products Sector Index (PHLX)

FVX.X 5-year Treasury Note Index	GTX Goldman Sachs Commodity/Total Return
GAX.X Gaming Index (CBOE)	
GHA.X GSTI Hardware Index (CBOE)	GVX Goldman Sachs Commodity/Livestock
GIN.X GSTI Internet Index (CBOE)	GYX Goldman Sachs Commodity/Ind. Metals
GIP.X GSTI Multimedia Networking Index (CBOE)	HCX.X S&P Health Care Index (CBOE)
GJX Goldman Sachs Commodity/Energy	HFX.X SuperCap Sector Index (PHLX)
GKX Goldman Sachs Commodity/Agricultural	HHPA Handy Harmon Palladium Index {D30}
GNX Goldman Sachs Commodity Index	HHPL Handy Harmon Platinum Index {D30}
GPX Goldman Sachs Commodity/Prec. Metals	HKL.X Hong Kong Index (4% value)
GSM.X GSTI Semiconductor Index (CBOE)	HKO.X Hong Kong Option Index (AMEX)
GSO.X GSTI Software Index (CBOE)	HKX.X AMEX Hong Kong 30 Index
GSV.X GSTI Services Index (CBOE)	HMO.X Morgan Stanley Healthcare Payor Index (AMEX)
GTB.X Lehman Bros. Global Telecommunications Basket	
GTC.X GSTI Composite Index (CBOE)	IDX S&P 400 MidCap Index
	IIX.X AMEX Internet Index (AMEX)

INDSX NASDAQ Industrial Index	IXN.X NASDAQ New York Regional Index
INDU Dow Jones Industrial Average (sm)	IXS.X NASDAQ San Francisco Regional Index
INSRX NASDAQ Insurance Index	IXTCX NASDAQ Telecommunication Index
INX S&P 500 Index (CME)	
INX.X CBOE Internet Index (CBOE)	IXW.X NASDAQ Washington D.C. Regional Index
IRX.X 13-week Treasury Bill Index	IZC.X Implied forward rate for $IRX.X
IUS.X S&P Insurance Index Ex. Set. Value	IZD.X Implied forward rate for $IRX.X
IUX Russell 2000 Stock Index	
IUX.X S&P Insurance Index (CBOE)	IZE.X Implied forward rate for $IRX.X
IXA.X NASDAQ ADR Index	IZF.X Implied forward rate for $IRX.X
IXBTX NASDAQ Combined Biotechnology Index	IZG.X Implied forward rate for $IRX.X
IXC.X NASDAQ Chicago Regional Index	IZI.X Implied forward rate for $IRX.X
IXCOX NASDAQ Computer Index	
IXF.X NASDAQ Financial 100 Index	JEX.X CBOE Japan Export Index
IXK.X NASDAQ Oklahoma Regional Index	JPN.X Japan Index (AMEX)
	JPV.X $JPN.X Settlement Value
IXL.X NASDAQ Los Angeles Regional Index	LEX.X Long term Mexico Index

LNU.X Long term Nikkei 300 Index

LSY.X SPX.X Index Dec 94 LEAPS

LTX.X Latin 15 Index (CBOE)

MDO.X S&P MidCap 400 FLEX Option Set. Val. (o,c)

MEX.X Mexico Index (CBOE)

MIA.X S&P MidCap 400 FLEX Option Set. Val. (o,c,h,l)

MID.X S&P 400 MidCap Index (AMEX)

MIH.X S&P MidCap 400 FLEX Option Set. Val. (h,l)

MMX Major Market Index

MPE.X Midcap 400 SPDR Est Cash Acnt

MSH.X Morgan Stanley High-Technology 35 Index (AMEX)

MXN.X S&P MidCap 400 Net Asset Index

MXU.X Midcap 400 SPDR Tot Cash

MXV.X Midcap 400 SPDR U Trade

MXY.X Mexico Index (The) (AMEX)

MZS.X S&P 400 MidCap SPDR Shares Outstanding Index

NCMPX Composite for Natl. Mrkt. System

ND.X NYSE Industrial Index

NDX.X NASDAQ-100 Index (CBOE)

NF.X NYSE Financial Index

NHB.X NYSE Beta Index

NIK.X Nikkei 300 Index (CBOE)

NNA.X NYSE Utility Index

NNX.X NYSE Opening Settlement for Utility Index

NV.X NYSE Transportation Index

NYA.X NYSE Composite Index (CBOE)

NYX.X NYSE Opening Settlement for Composite Index

OAV.X OEX.X FLEX Average Set. and High/Low Value

OBX.X S&P 100 Index Dec 94 LEAPS

OCO.X OEX.X FLEX Average Exercise Set. Val.

OCS.X SPX.X FLEX Average Exercise Set. Val.	RIX.X REIT Index (CBOE)
OET.X OEX.X FLEX Opening Exercise Set. Val.	RLS.X RUT.X FLEX Opening Ex. Set. Value
OEX S&P 100 Index (CME)	RLX.X S&P Retail Index (CBOE)
OEX.X S&P 100 Index (CBOE)	RMS.X Morg Stanley REIT Index
OEZ.X S&P 100 Index Amer. Sty. Index	RRS.X S&P Retail Index Ex. Set. Value
OFINX NASDAQ Finance Index	RSI.X REIT Index Final Settlement
OGS.X S&P MidCap OSG Shares Ex Index	RUA.X Russell 3000 Index
	RUI.X Russell 1000 Index
OHL.X OEX.X FLEX Average High/Low Value	RUT.X Russell 2000 Index (CBOE)
ORC.X RUT.X FLEX Avg. Exercise Set. Val.	RUV.X FLEX Avg. Set. and High/Low Value
PLN.X Airline Sector Index (PHLX)	RXH.X Morgan Stanley Healthcare Provider (AMEX)
PNX.X Phone Sector Index (PHLX)	RXP.X Morgan Stanley Healthcare Product Index (AMEX)
PON.X Airline Index Final Set. Val.	
POX.X Phone Sector Index Settlement	SAV.X FLEX Avg. Set. and High/Low Value
PSE.X PSE Technology 100 Index (PACX)	SET.X $SPX.X FLEX Opening Ex. Set. Value
RHL.X $RUT.X FLEX Avg. High/Low Value	SGX.X S&P 500/BARRA Growth Index (CBOE)

SHL.X $SPX.X FLEX Average High/Low Value	SXS.X SPDRs Shares Outstanding
SML.X S&P SmallCap 600 Index (CBOE)	SXV.X SPDRs Underlying Trading Value
SOX.X Semiconductor Sector Index (PHLX)	TCX.X CBOE Telecommunications Index
SPE.X SPDRs Estimated Cash Account	TICK NYSE Issues up—issues down
SPL.X S&P 500 Index—Long-Term (CBOE)	TIKI Dow Jones Industrial issues up—issues down
SPQ.X S&P 500 End-of-Quarter	TNS.X 10-year Treasury Note Index Settlement
SPU.X SPDRs Creation Unit Total Cash Amount	TNX.X 10-year Treasury Note Index
SPX.X S&P 500 Index (CBOE)	TOP.X Eurotop 100 Index
SPZ.X S&P 500 Index strike price overflow	TPX.X U.S. Top 100 Index (PHLX)
SSX.X 13-week Treasury Bill Index Settlement	TPX.X U.S. Top 100 Index (PHLX)
SVX.X S&P 500/BARRA Value Index (CBOE)	TRAN Dow Jones Transportation Average
SXD.X SPDRs Net Accumulated Dividend	TRANX NASDAQ Transportation Index
SXN.X SPDRs Net Asset Value	TRIN NYSE Short Term Trading Index (Arms Index)
SXP.X SPDRs Final Quarterly Dividend	

TRS.X S&P Transportation Index Ex. Set. Value	XAX.X AMEX Composite
TRX.X S&P Transportation Index (CBOE)	XBD.X Securities Broker/Dealer Index (The) (AMEX)
TXX.X Technology Index (CBOE)	XBS.X Securities Broker Dealer Index
TYS.X 30-year Treasury Bond Index Settlement	XCB.X Bear Stearns CONS Prtf Basket
TYX.X 30-year Treasury Bond Index	XCI.X Computer Technology Index (AMEX)
UTIL Dow Jones Utilities Average	XFI.X AMEX Financial Sub-Index
UTY.X Utility Sector Index (PHLX)	XHL.X AMEX Healthcare Sub-Index
VIX.X Market Volatility Index (CBOE)	XIA.X Institutional Index FLEX Option Set. Val. (o,c,h,l)
VLE.X Value Line Composite Index (PHLX)	XID.X AMEX Industrial Sub-Index
WSX.X Wilshire Small Cap Index (PACX)	XIH.X Institutional Index FLEX Option Set. Val. (h,l)
XAL.X Airline Index (AMEX)	XII.X Institutional Index (AMEX)
XAO.X AMEX Airlines Index Final Settlement	XIO.X Institutional Index FLEX Option Set. Val. (o,c)
XAT.X Market Value Idx Mid Atlantic	XIT.X AMEX Information Technologies Sub-Index
XAU.X Gold and Silver Sector Index (PHLX)	XMA.X Major Market Index FLEX Option Set. Val. (o,c,h,l)

XMH.X Major Market Index FLEX Option Set. Val. (h,l)	XOI.X Oil Index (AMEX)
XMI.X Major Market Index (AMEX)	XSV.X XILX Settlement Valuation
XMO.X Major Market Index FLEX Option Set. Val. (o,c)	XTC.X North American Telecommunications Index (AMEX)
XMV.X Major Market Index FLEX Option Set. Val. (o,c)	XTV.X XTC.X Settlement Valuation
XNG.X Natural Gas Index (The) (AMEX)	XVL.X Value Line Index 1/10Th
XOC.X National Over-The-Counter Sector Index	ZRU.X Long Term Russell 2000 Index 97

U.S. Stock Sector Indexes

DGL.X DRG.X LEAPS Index	DJR.X Dow Jones Equity REIT Index (CBOE)
XAL.X Airline Index (AMEX)	
IIX.X AMEX Internet Index (AMEX)	ECM.X Dow Jones Internet Commerce Index (CBOE)
AUX.X Automotive Index (CBOE)	FPP.X Forest & Paper Products Sector Index (PHLX)
BTK.X Biotechnology Index (AMEX)	GAX.X Gaming Index (CBOE)
BKL.X BTK LEAPS Index	XAU.X Gold and Silver Sector Index (PHLX)
INX.X CBOE Internet Index (CBOE)	HUI.X Gold BUGS Index (AMEX)
BMX.X Computer Box Maker Sector Index (PHLX)	GTC.X GSTI Composite Index (CBOE)
CWX.X Computer Software Index (CBOE)	GHA.X GSTI Hardware Index (CBOE)
XCI.X Computer Technology Index (AMEX)	GIN.X GSTI Internet Index (CBOE)
CTN.X CSFB Technology Index (AMEX)	GIP.X GSTI Multimedia Networking Index (CBOE)
YTK.X de Jager Year 2000 Index	GSM.X GSTI Semiconductor Index (CBOE)
DXE.X Deutsche Bank Energy Index (AMEX)	GSV.X GSTI Services Index (CBOE)
DDX.X Disk Drive Index (AMEX)	GSO.X GSTI Software Index (CBOE)
MUT.X Dow 10 Index (CBOE)	

XII.X Institutional Index (AMEX)	IXL.X NASDAQ Los Angeles Regional Index
BKX.X KBW Bank Sector Index (PHLX)	IXN.X NASDAQ New York Regional Index
GTB.X Lehman Bros. Global Telecommunications Basket	IXS.X NASDAQ San Francisco Regional Index
EGI.X Morgan Stanley Emerging Growth Index (PACX)	IXTCX NASDAQ Telecommunication Index
HMO.X Morgan Stanley Healthcare Payor Index (AMEX)	TRANX NASDAQ Transportation Index
RXP.X Morgan Stanley Healthcare Product Index (AMEX)	IXW.X NASDAQ Washington D.C. Regional Index
RXH.X Morgan Stanley Healthcare Provider (AMEX)	XNG.X Natural Gas Index (The) (AMEX)
MSH.X Morgan Stanley High-Technology 35 Index (AMEX)	NWX.X Networking Index (The) (AMEX)
BANKX NASDAQ Banking Index	XTC.X North American Telecommunications Index (AMEX)
IXC.X NASDAQ Chicago Regional Index	NF.X NYSE Financial Index
IXBTX NASDAQ Combined Biotechnology Index	ND.X NYSE Industrial Index
IXCOX NASDAQ Computer Index	NV.X NYSE Transportation Index
OFINX NASDAQ Finance Index	NNA.X NYSE Utility Index
IXF.X NASDAQ Financial 100 Index	XOI.X Oil Index (AMEX)
INSRX NASDAQ Insurance Index	OIX.X Oil Index (CBOE)

OSX.X Oil Service Sector Index (PHLX)	XBS.X Securities Broker Dealer Index
OTX.X OTC Prime Sector Index (PHLX)	XBD.X Securities Broker/Dealer Index (The) (AMEX)
DRG.X Pharmaceutical Index (AMEX)	SOX.X Semiconductor Sector Index (PHLX)
PNX.X Phone Sector Index (PHLX)	HFX.X SuperCap Sector Index (PHLX)
PSE.X PSE Technology 100 Index (PACX)	TXX.X Technology Index (CBOE)
BIX.X S&P Banks Index (CBOE)	HWI.X The Computer Hardware Index (AMEX)
CEX.X S&P Chemical Index (CBOE)	DOT.X TheStreet.com Internet Sector Index (PHLX)
HCX.X S&P Health Care Index (CBOE)	ICX.X TheStreet.com E-commerce Index
IUX.X S&P Insurance Index (CBOE)	UTY.X Utility Sector Index (PHLX)
RLX.X S&P Retail Index (CBOE)	
TRX.X S&P Transportation Index (CBOE)	

Semiconductor Index SOX.X Stocks ranked by volume

BRCM Broadcom Corporation 46305000	AMCC Applied Micro Circuits Corporation 4769400
INTC Intel Corporation 20715600	ADI Analog Devices Inc 4613900
TXN Texas Instrs Inc 8848800	CNXT Conexant Systems, Inc. 4335200
RMBS Rambus, Inc. 7686600	
AMAT Applied Materials, Inc. 7476100	AMKR Amkor Technology, Inc. 4075700
LRCX Lam Research Corporation 7427100	ALTR Altera Corporation 3973300
	SDLI SDL, Inc. 3873700
MU Micron Technology Inc 6646400	LLTC Linear Technology Corporation 3773800
XLNX Xilinx, Inc. 6631300	CY Cypress Semiconductor Corp 3703500
LSI LSI Logic Corp 6171600	
IDTI Integrated Device Technology, Inc. 5497200	PMCS PMC—Sierra, Inc. 3634600
AMD Advanced Micro Devices Inc 5208600	TQNT TriQuint Semiconductor, Inc. 3439900
SSTI Silicon Storage Technology, Inc. 5063500	NSM National Semiconductor Corp 3225500
NVDA NVIDIA Corporation 5038600	NVLS Novellus Systems, Inc. 3202800
MXIM Maxim Integrated Products, Inc. 5009700	MRVC MRV Communications, Inc. 3068300

RFMD RF Micro Devices, Inc. 3064100	OAKT Oak Technology, Inc. 1719200
AHAA Alpha Industries, Inc. 2748700	ANAD ANADIGICS, Inc. 1681600
VTSS Vitesse Semiconductor Corporation 2743700	ISSI Integrated Silicon Solution, Inc. 1674200
STLW Stratos Lightwave, Inc. 2542700	IRF International Rectifier Corp 1673700
FLEX Flextronics International Ltd. 2507500	SMTC Semtech Corporation 1569700
ALSC Alliance Semiconductor Corporation 2470700	CREE Cree, Inc. 1459800
QLGC QLogic Corporation 2424600	DS Dallas Semiconductor Corp 1429900
MCRL Micrel, Incorporated 2352200	LTXX LTX Corporation 1318600
	TLCM TelCom Semiconductor, Inc. 1208800
BBRC Burr-Brown Corporation 2338400	VRTA Virata Corporation 1171700
CMOS Credence Systems Corporation 1966200	ELNT Elantec Semiconductor, Inc. 1106500
LSCC Lattice Semiconductor Corporation 1878800	TSM Taiwan Semiconductor Mfg Co 1106100
GSPN GlobeSpan, Inc. 1789500	GALT Galileo Technology Ltd. 1067700
TXCC TranSwitch Corporation 1787700	SIMG Silicon Image, Inc. 1066200

CUBE C-Cube Microsystems Inc. 1030500

ASML ASM Lithography Holding N.V. 1027700

ASYT Asyst Technologies, Inc. 1005300

CRUS Cirrus Logic, Inc. 963200

SFAM SpeedFam-IPEC Inc. 955500

MCHP Microchip Technology Incorporated 944200

ETEK E-Tek Dynamics, Inc. 921800

NMGC NeoMagic Corporation 919500

PHTN Photon Dynamics, Inc. 893600

MRVL Marvell Technology Group, Ltd. 879500

TFS Three-Five Systems, Inc. 865500

ONNN SCG Holding Corporation ON Semiconductor 851400

ISIL Intersil Holding Corporation 840900

FCS Fairchild Semiconductor Intl 830900

PSEM Pericom Semiconductor Corporation 802000

ACTL Actel Corporation 801800

SYMM Symmetricom, Inc. 776100

VSEA Varian Semiconductor Equipment Associates, Inc. 741300

LPTHA LightPath Technologies, Inc. 734200

CHRT Chartered Semiconductor Manufacturing Ltd. 730400

UTCI Uniroyal Technology Corporation 705100

STM Stmicroelectronics N V 696000

ZRAN Zoran Corporation 693300

QUIK QuickLogic Corporation 690400

FEIC FEI Company 658500

ICST Integrated Circuit Systems, Inc. 648800

MTSN Mattson Technology, Inc. 640900

MSCC Microsemi Corporation 621800	FSII FSI International, Inc. 524000
TGAL Tegal Corporation 559600	PLXT PLX Technology, Inc. 510700
AVNX Avanex Corporation 557200	ARXX Aeroflex Incorporated 505500
PXLW Pixelworks, Inc. 555800	SMTL Semitool, Inc. 495300
ASMI ASM International N.V. 554100	BRKS Brooks Automation, Inc. 492600
KLIC Kulicke and Soffa Industries, Inc. 537800	SILI Siliconix Incorporated 465700
EGLS Electroglas, Inc. 531200	SUPX Supertex, Inc. 448800

Software Index CWX.X Stocks ranked by volume

MSFT Microsoft Corporation 26178200	PMTC Parametric Technology Corporation 5144400
ORCL Oracle Corporation 19046500	PSFT PeopleSoft, Inc. 4608200
BVSN BroadVision, Inc. 10395800	TIBX TIBCO Software, Inc. 4374300
IFMX Informix Corporation 10117400	RHAT Red Hat, Inc. 4360800
FTRL FutureLink Corp. 8292800	VRSN VeriSign, Inc. 4021400
VRTS VERITAS Software Corporation 7966700	PRSF Portal Software, Inc. 4002900
BEAS BEA Systems, Inc. 7489800	ITRU Intertrust Technologies Corporation 3989100
CMRC Commerce One, Inc. 6774400	SYBS Sybase, Inc. 3903700
CPWR Compuware Corporation 6143100	BMCS BMC Software, Inc. 3900900
VIGN Vignette Corporation 6018600	MERQ Mercury Interactive Corporation 3605400
MSTR MicroStrategy Incorporated 5518500	PRGN Peregrine Systems, Inc. 3257500
ARBA Ariba, Inc. 5264600	EGAN eGain Communications Corporation 3135000
CTXS Citrix Systems, Inc. 5191700	BBSW Broadbase Software, Inc. 3120600
	SEBL Siebel Systems, Inc. 3115700

VIAN Viant Corporation 3104900	CHKP Check Point Software Technologies, Ltd. 2206900
PUMA Puma Technology, Inc. 3042100	RNWK RealNetworks, Inc. 2191100
LGTO Legato Systems, Inc. 2860100	SBAS StarBase Corporation 2162400
INTU Intuit Inc. 2850600	ACRU Accrue Software, Inc. 2132800
LBRT Liberate Technologies 2848500	RATL Rational Software Corporation 2048900
JDEC J.D. Edwards & Company 2810500	AVNT Avant! Corporation 1992200
ITWO i2 Technologies, Inc. 2739600	NETM NetManage, Inc. 1880700
ARTG Art Technology Group, Inc. 2651500	ISSX ISS Group, Inc. 994600
PHCM Phone.com, Inc. 2588100	AETH Aether Systems, Inc. 984200
SGNT Sagent Technology, Inc. 2536800	MDRX Allscripts, Inc. 973800
KANA Kana Communications, Inc. 2481100	BVEW Bindview Development Corp 972700
CA Computer Associate Intl Inc 2399100	OMKT Open Market, Inc. 960800
GMGC General Magic, Inc. 2366400	NAVR Navarre Corporation 959100
VITR Vitria Technology, Inc. 2288100	RSAS RSA Security, Inc. 956500
	MUSE Micromuse, Inc. 956300

NETO NetObjects, Inc. 936000	PRSW Persistence Software, Inc. 753300
SSSW SilverStream Software, Inc. 932400	PKSI Primus Knowledge Solutions, Inc. 751200
DCTI Digital Courier Technologies, Inc. 909300	CORL Corel Corporation 748600
ELON Echelon Corporation 889000	RETK Retek Inc. 747700
MCRE MetaCreations Corporation 866600	ADVS Advent Software, Inc. 743800
CYCH CyberCash, Inc. 850700	CHRZ Computer Horizons Corp. 737800
NETE Netegrity, Inc. 813700	MENT Mentor Graphics Corporation 735000
FIRE FirePond, Inc. 805800	MPLX Mediaplex, Inc. 731800
TTWO Take-Two Interactive Software, Inc. 798100	OSII Objective Systems Integrators, Inc. 724900
EXLN eXcelon Corporation 790100	VIAD Viador Inc. 718100
ERTS Electronic Arts Inc. 789800	SAP SAP Ag 609700
PVSW Pervasive Software Inc. 783700	LNTE Lante Corporation 609100
MAPX MAPICS Inc. 771800	INTD InteliData Technologies Corporation 1862500
WGRD WatchGuard Technologies, Inc. 770000	ASPT Aspect Communications Corporation 1845800
QMDC QuadraMed Corporation 762400	CLRN Clarent Corporation 1763900
	LTWO Learn2.com Inc. 1744500

INPR Inprise Corporation 1681300	CLRS Clarus Corporation 1385000
SONE S1 Corporation 1675600	VNWK Visual Networks, Inc. 1377000
IWOV Interwoven, Inc. 1654500	AGIL Agile Software Corporation 1359100
MMGR Medical Manager Corporation 1651900	ENTU Entrust Technologies, Inc. 1350300
WIND Wind River Systems, Inc. 1641100	NETA Network Associates, Inc. 1344600
IMAN iManage, Inc. 1608900	ASWX Active Software, Inc. 1324900
SCUR Secure Computing Corporation 1596000	INTW InterWorld Corporation 1305700
AKLM Acclaim Entertainment, Inc. 1589400	VRGE Virage, Inc. 1294900
ALLR Allaire Corporation 1496300	MESG MessageMedia Inc. 1293800
INCX InfoCure Corporation 1493800	ADBE Adobe Systems Incorporated 1276800
USIX USinternetworking, Inc. 1485600	NEON New Era Networks, Inc. 1272100
ASTN Ashton Technology Group, Inc. (The) 1476500	IRIC Information Resources, Inc. 1252600
SNPS Synopsys, Inc. 1470100	CLIC Calico Commerce, Inc. 1249500
BYND Beyond.com Corporation 1455100	EPNY E.piphany, Inc. 1248200
QNTS Quintus Corporation 1445000	

CDN Cadence Designs Sys Inc 1220500	BLSW Bluestone Software, Inc. 996400
EPIC Epicor Software Corporation 1217700	PXCM Proxicom, Inc. 601800
IARC Information Architects Corporation 1207200	CWLD CrossWorlds Software, Inc. 600800VRTY Verity, Inc. 704600
SYMC Symantec Corporation 1198700	INTF Interface Systems, Inc. 700100
NTIQ NetIQ Corporation 1191600	IN Infonet Svcs Corp 696200
SWCM Software.com, Inc. 1144100	SQSW Sequoia Software Corporation 694800
ENGA Engage, Inc. 1124300	UNFY Unify Corporation 692100
TMWD Tumbleweed Communications Corp. 1121100	MANU Manugistics Group, Inc. 668700
EFII Electronics for Imaging, Inc. 1107400	MDLI MedicaLogic/Medscape Inc 663800
RAMP Ramp Networks, Inc. 1080000	MCTR Mercator Software Inc 661700
INKT Inktomi Corporation 1043700	MACR Macromedia, Inc. 654500
SCOC Santa Cruz Operation, Inc. (The) 1030300	NIKU Niku Corporation 649200
	PTEC Phoenix Technologies Ltd. 648100
THDO 3DO Company (The) 1030200	SOFO Sonic Foundry, Inc. 644700
	CHRD Chordiant Software, Inc. 643500

TANN Tanning Technology Corporation 642200 PSDI Project Software & Development, Inc. 631800 MSLV MetaSolv Software, Inc. 628000 ATVI Activision, Inc. 619700 DRTE Dendrite International, Inc. 612500DALN Daleen Technologies, Inc. 599100 SEAC SeaChange International, Inc. 578600 HYSL Hyperion Solutions Corporation 565300 INFA Informatica Corporation 538300	DRIV Digital River, Inc. 536800 AREM AremisSoft Corporation 535300 PEGA Pegasystems Inc. 528600 DCTM Documentum, Inc. 526400 AVTC AVT Corporation 521900 DOX Amdocs Ltd 512900 DSET DSET Corporation 509200 SDRC Structural Dynamics Research Corporation 508700 RMDY Remedy Corporation 504400

Computer Networking Index NWX.X
Stocks ranked by volume

CSCO Cisco Systems, Inc. 34402600	NYFX NYFIX, Inc. 946200
COMS 3Com Corporation 15847800	JKHY Jack Henry & Associates, Inc. 785100
BRCD Brocade Communications Systems, Inc. 4383800	INRS IntraNet Solutions Inc. 757300
NTAP Network Appliance, Inc. 4318200	REY Reynolds & Reynolds Co 748700
NOVL Novell, Inc. 3093900	PILL ProxyMed, Inc. 736500
ACCD Accord Networks, Inc. 2341000	GBIX Globix Corporation 709100
NTRX Netrix Corporation 2221900	ANET ACT Networks, Inc. 679400
FFIV F5 Networks, Inc. 1437800	SYKE Sykes Enterprises, Incorporated 582300
CVG Convergys Corp 1271600	AFFI Affinity Technology Group, Inc. 515200
VRTL Vertel Corporation 1255000	NTCT NetScout Systems, Inc. 515200
TTN Titan Corp 1155900	INTZ Intrusion.com Inc 502600
TLXN Telxon Corporation 1116600	TSCC Technology Solutions Company 462200
CFLO CacheFlow Inc. 971600	
PSIX PSINet Inc. 948200	

Computer Hardware Index XCI.X
Stocks ranked by volume

CPQ Compaq Computer Corp 26587700	MIPS MIPS Technologies, Inc. 987600
DELL Dell Computer Corporation 21553100	TECD Tech Data Corporation 961700
PALM Palm, Inc. 16396500	NCDI Network Computing Devices, Inc. 812800
IBM International Business Machines Corp 8612600	ASPX Auspex Systems, Inc. 812600
SUNW Sun Microsystems, Inc. 8607100	LNUX VA Linux Systems, Inc. 659100
AAPL Apple Computer, Inc. 5769600	CCUR Concurrent Computer Corporation 590800
HWP Hewlett Packard Co 4265500	MUEI Micron Electronics, Inc. 480400
SGI Silicon Graphics Inc 3711700	IM Ingram Micro Inc. 389500
COBT Cobalt Networks, Inc. 3598800	MXWL Maxwell Technologies, Inc. 288900
GTW Gateway Inc. 2627100	MRCY Mercury Computer Systems 229300
MSEL Merisel, Inc. 1472700	
XYBR Xybernaut Corporation 1257600	BTWS Bitwise Designs, Inc. 124000
HAND Handspring, Inc. 1243500	CRAY Cray Inc 121700
EEEE eMachines, Inc. 1008500	ASPE Aspeon Inc 117900

ATEC ATEC Group Inc. 69600 SVTG Savoir Technology Group, Inc. 67900 VTCH Vitech America, Inc. 63000 DGII Digi International Inc. 58500 FWRX FieldWorks, Inc. 56600	BWSI Blue Wave Systems Inc. 56500 NWRE Neoware Systems Inc. 48300 HIT Hitachi Ltd 47700 PERL Perle Systems Limited 43900

Communications Equipment Index XTC.X
Stocks ranked by volume

QCOM QUALCOMM Incorporated 18508100	CIEN CIENA Corporation 4007300
ERICY LM Ericsson Telephone Company 17474200	FNSR Finisar Corporation 3582800
MOT Motorola Inc. 15622800	NTRO Netro Corporation 3565300
NOK Nokia Corp 14766500	
JDSU JDS Uniphase Corporation 13581900	ANDW Andrew Corporation 3218700
NT Nortel Networks Corp. 11464700	DMIC Digital Microwave Corporation 2607200
JNPR Juniper Networks 9978800	ICOM Intelect Communications, Inc. 2551300
LU Lucent Technologies Inc 9754700	FDRY Foundry Networks, Inc. 2468400
SCMR Sycamore Networks, Inc. 7867000	GLW Corning Inc 2182700
ADCT ADC Telecommunications, Inc. 5948500	PWAV Powerwave Technologies, Inc. 2151000
HLIT Harmonic Inc. 5544200	TERN Terayon Communication Systems, Inc. 1960200
AFCI Advanced Fibre Communications 4329600	CLST Cellstar Corporation 1935100
TLAB Tellabs, Inc. 4191500	CMVT Comverse Technology, Inc. 1909300

CMTN Copper Mountain Networks, Inc. 1893300	CAMP California Amplifier, Inc. 1213400
DIGL Digital Lightwave, Inc. 1693200	VG Viasystems Group Inc 1195400
SFA Scientific Atlanta Inc 1657000	ADTN ADTRAN, Inc. 1117800
ALA Alcatel Alsthom Inc 1648700	TLGD Tollgrade Communications, Inc. 1057900
TKLC Tekelec 1594500	ATON Alteon WebSystems, Inc. 1002800
SMRA Somera Communications, Inc. 1453400	NMSS Natural MicroSystems Corporation 990700
EFNT Efficient Networks, Inc. 1418700	CTV Commscope Inc 976600
PDYN Paradyne Networks, Inc. 1416900	ADAP Adaptive Broadband Corporation 931900
LOR Loral Space & Communications 1394300	BIGT Pinnacle Holdings, Inc. 919700
WAVO WAVO Corporation, Inc. 1389200	WINK Wink Communications 849900
PCTL PictureTel Corporation 1375600	CMTO Com21, Inc. 810100
DITC Ditech Communications Corporation 1294900	ACCL Accelerated Networks, Inc. 798200
PLCM Polycom, Inc. 1279700	SNWL SonicWALL, Inc. 784200
WSTL Westell Technologies, Inc. 1225800	IATV ACTV Inc. 771000
	PCTI PC-Tel, Inc. 737900
	DAVX Davox Corporation 718000

INTL Inter-Tel, Incorporated 716200	ANEN Anaren Microwave, Inc. 554700
VSAT ViaSat, Inc. 680200	CLTK Celeritek, Inc. 550500
REMC REMEC, Inc. 632300	CELL Brightpoint, Inc. 514200
CCBL C-COR.net Corporation 620400	INTV InterVoice-Brite, Inc. 506200
GEMS Glenayre Technologies, Inc. 605500	VYYO Vyyo, Inc. 505800
	ADSX Applied Digital Solutions, Inc. 505000
AXC Ampex Corporation 598300	
ONIS ONI Systems Corp. 596200	ORCT Orckit Communications, Limited 443800
FIBR Osicom Technologies, Inc. 561700	
	LUMM Lumenon Innovative Lightwave Technology, Inc. 442400
RACE DATA RACE, Inc. 555900	
NXTV Next Level Communications, Inc. 555300	

Dow Jones 30 Stocks INDU

AA Alcoa Inc.	HD Home Depot Inc
ALD Allied Signal Inc	INTC Intel Corporation
AXP American Express Co	IBM International Business Machines Corp
T AT&T Corp	
BA Boeing Co	IP International Paper Co
CAT Caterpillar Inc	JNJ Johnson & Johnson
C Citigroup Inc	MCD Mcdonalds Corp
KO Coca Cola Co	MRK Merck & Co Inc
DIS The Walt Disney Company	MSFT Microsoft Corporation
DD Du Pont E I De Nemours & Co	MMM Minnesota Mng & Mfg Co
	JPM Morgan J P & Co Inc
EK Eastman Kodak Co	MO Philip Morris Cos Inc
XON Exxon Corp	PG Procter & Gamble Co
GE General Electric Co.	SBC SBC Communications Inc.
GM General Motors Corp.	UTX United Technologies Corp
HWP Hewlett Packard Co	WMT Wal Mart Stores Inc

TC2000 scans for short term trading

1) Stocks With Good Volume And Closed At High For The day.

On the toolbar click on Databank

Click on Personal Criteria Formulas.

Click on the Create New button.

Type in Closed at high w/good Volume.

Click on the OK button.

In the Formula box type (C = H) AND (V > 5000)

Click the Save Button.

In the calculate for box on the bottom of the Personal Criteria Formulas box, make sure that it reads "All Items In System".

Click the Close Button.

Click the Yes Button.

Note. When Writing TC2000 volume scans leave off the last two zeros for a volume number i.e. 5000 will be 500,000

2) Trend Reversal Gap And Closed At The High.

On the toolbar click on Databank.

Click on Personal Criteria Formulas.

Click on the Create New button.

Type in Trend Reversal Gap

Click on the OK button.

In the Formula box type:

(C60 > C40) AND (C40 > C20) AND (C20 > C5) AND (C2 > C1) AND (O > C1) AND (L > C1) AND (C = H) AND (V > 5000)

Click the Save Button.

In the calculate for box on the bottom of the Personal Criteria Formulas box, make sure that it reads "All Items In System".

Click the Close Button.
Click the Yes Button.

Note. This is a specialized scan and may not turn up candidates everyday.

3) **Good Intra day Volatility With Strong Volume.**
On the toolbar click on Databank
Click on Personal Criteria Formulas.
Click on the Create New button.
Type in High Intra day Range w/good volume
Click on the OK button
In the Formula box type
(AVGH5—AVGL5 > 3.00) AND (AVGV5 > 7500)
Click the Save Button.
In the calculate for box on the bottom of the Personal Criteria
Formulas box, make sure that it reads "All Items In System".
Click the Close Button.
Click the Yes Button.

Glossary

Glossary of Terms

Amateur Hour: Refers to the first hour of market trading when individuals trade. Institutions generally trade in last hour of market trading.

AMEX: The American Stock Exchange

Ax: The lead market maker on a stock. The market maker who has the ability to manipulate a stocks movement.

Bid and Ask: Bid is the price in which a retail trader buys a stock at and the Ask is the price in which a retail trader sells the stock at.

Buy To Open: A buy to order is placed when buying a stock that you currently have no position in.

Buy To Close: A buy order placed to close a position. Used to close a short position.

Buying Power: The amount of money you have available in your account to purchase stocks.

Cash Account: An account that has no margin abilities. Used for stocks and options.

CBOE: Chicago Board of Options Exchange.

Day Order: An Order that will expire at the close of the trading day unless it is filled.

Day trader: A trader who closes every transaction by the end of each day.

DOW: Dow Jones 30. 30 of Americas largest companies.

DSL: Dedicated Subscriber line providing a quick, always on Internet connection.

Earnings Run: The period just before a stock announces their quarterly earnings. If the stock starts to increase in price with heavy buying during this time it is called an earnings run.

ECN: Electronic Communication Network. An ECN is a trading platform that allows an individual trader direct access to the markets. Trading through an ECN gives a trader the ability to buy at the Bid and sell at the Ask.

Economic Indicator: Economic Numbers released throughout the month gauging the strength of the overall economy.

EPS: Earnings Per Share.

Fading The Trend: A market maker who sits at the inside bid or ask and does not move with the intention of stopping a stock or reversing a stocks direction is Fading The Trend.

Fed Call: A margin Call that can't be cleared up by selling assets to cover the difference. With a Fed Call, a trader must send in additional funds to cover the call.

Form 10-K: An annual report, which provides a comprehensive overview of the company for the past year. The filing is due 90 days after the close of the company's fiscal year, and contains such information as company history, organization, nature of business, equity, holdings, earnings per share, subsidiaries, and other pertinent financial information.

Form 10-Q: A quarterly report, which provides a continuing view of a company's financial position during the year. The filing is due 45 days after each of the first three fiscal quarters. No filing is due for the fourth quarter.

Form 144: This form must be filed by "insiders" prior to their intended sale of restricted stock (issued stock currently unregistered with the SEC). Filing this form results in each seller receiving an automatic exemption from SEC registration requirements for this one transaction. 144 sales frequently come in clusters caused by events such as the end of a "lock-up" period or stock options being exercised and can be used to successfully project the onset of increased "sell side" activity in the stock of the target company.

Form 3: An initial filing of equity securities filed by every director, officer, or owner of more than ten percent of a class of equity securities. Contains information on the reporting person's relationship to the company and on purchases and sales of equity securities. This form type is not required to be filed with the EDGAR system.

Form 4: Any changes to a Form 3 are made here.

Form Def 14A: Provides official notification to designated classes of shareholders of matters to be brought to a vote at a shareholders meeting. This form is commonly referred to as a "Proxy".

Form Pre 14A: A preliminary proxy statement providing official notification to designated classes of shareholders of matters to be brought to a vote at a shareholders meeting

Form S-4: A filing for the registration of securities for a business transaction.

Form S-8: A filing for securities that are to be offered to employees pursuant to employee benefit plans.

Form SC 13D: This filing is made by person(s) reporting beneficially owned shares of common stock in a public company.

Form SC 13G: A statement of beneficial ownership of common stock by certain persons.

Full Service Broker: A broker who handles and recommends trades for a client's account. Generally a full service broker will charge higher commissions and want to be a buy and hold investor.

Gap: When a stock closes at one price and open the next morning at another price.

Gap and Trap: A play in which a market maker gaps a stock up at the open to fill market orders and lull buyers in and then immediately lowers the price trapping traders at a loss.

GTC: Good Till Canceled. A standing order to buy or sell that is good until it is canceled, filled or expires. Most GTC's are good for 60 days.

Head Fake: A play in which a market maker will quickly reverse a stocks direction to shake out traders from their position.

Index: An Index consists of a group of sectors. Watching an Index is a good way to gauge the overall pressure out on a sector or stock.

Inside Bid and Ask: The best bid and best ask price being displayed.

Instinet: A trading network originally designed for large institutions now available for all traders. Shown as INCA on a level II screen.

Institutional Traders: Large accounts, usually a pension or mutual fund.

Internet Broker: A brokerage firm that accepts buy and sell orders over the Internet.

Island: A trading network that allows traders direct access to the markets. The island network allow traders to buy at the bid and sell at the ask. Shown as ISLD on a level II screen.

ISP: Internet Service Provider.

Level I: A level I quote shows the bid price and best ask price on a stock.

Level II: A level II screen shows all market makers and ECN's making a market in a stock along with their bid ask quote and the share each are willing to buy or sell.

Level III: Same as a level II screen but allows market makers the ability to change, update or refresh their prices.

Limit Order: An order to buy or sell that specifies a limit amount that you are willing to buy or sell at.

MACD's: *M*oving *A*verage *C*onvergence *D*ivergence. A technical buy and sell signal.

Margin: Money borrowed from your broker allowing you to double your buying power.

Margin Account: A trading Account that allows you to double your buying power by using both yours and your broker's money.

Margin Call: A call to add more money to your account to cover a position or to liquidate some positions to free up capital.

Market Maker: A person who makes a two sided market on a Nasdaq stock. Market makers will trade in their own account and also fill orders for their clients.

Market Order: An order to buy or sell at any price. A market order is placed when you are looking for a quick fill but do not care at what price you are filled.

Moving Average: A technical buy and sell signal from a moving average line created from a stocks position over a period of time.

NASDAQ: National Association of Securities Dealers Automated Quotation.

NYSE: New York Stock Exchange

OEX: Standard & Poors 100 Index.

Option Account: A trading account for trading options.

OTC: Over The Counter. Stocks traded on the Nasdaq exchange are called Over The Counter stocks.

OTCBB: Over The Counter Bulletin Board. Small stocks traded on the Nasdaq exchange that are usually under $5.00 and light on volume.

Position trader: A short term trader who is generally in and out of a position in a couple days to a couple weeks.

Regulation T Call: A type of margin call that requires you to send in cash to cover a position.

Resistance Line: A price point above the current stock price that a stock could or does have a problem breaking through.

S&P Futures: Standard & Poors Futures. A basket of stocks traded 24 hours a day except for weekends and holidays. Used as a gauge to measure the strength of the open.

S.E.C.: Securities and Exchange Commission. A regulatory board for the U.S. stock exchanges.

S.O.E.S.: Small Order Execution System. A trading system that allows traders quick access to buy and sell fills.

Scalp: To take a small profit on a stock 1/16 to 1/8.

Sector: A grouping of similar stocks.

SelectNet: A trading system that allows a trader to send a buy or sell order to a specific market maker.

Sell To Close: A sell order placed to close out a position you are already in.

Sell To Open: A sell order placed to open a position. Used to open up a short position.

Shadowing: Copying the movements of the Ax.

Short Account: An account that allows a trader to short stocks.

Short Interest: The amount of shares on a stock that have been sold short and not yet been bought back to cover.

Short Squeeze: When a stock with heavy short interest announces positive news causing short sellers to quickly buy to cover their position and quickly pushing the stocks price up.

Shorting: Selling a security that you do not own.

Slam: The expression used when a stock loses at least 10% of its value in one day.

Slippage: The difference between the filled price on an order and the quoted price at the time of a fill.

Specialist: The individual who is responsible filling orders on a stock traded on the NYSE and AMEX.

Spread: The difference between the bid and ask price.

SPX: Standard & Poors 500 Index.

Stochastics: A technical buy and sell indicator caused when two averages cross. Stochastics are derived from orders filled at the bid and orders filled at the ask.

Stop Loss: An order to close out a position in case it turns against you.

SuperDot: Super Designated Order Turnaround. A computer system used on the NYSE to match and fill orders.

Support Line: A price point below the current stock price that a stock could or does have a problem breaking through.

T + 1 Rule: Trade day plus one additional trading day.

T + 3 Rule: Trade day plus three additional trading days.

Technical Indicator: A buy or sell indicator derived from a mathematical formula.

Teenies: 1/16 of a point.

Time Of Sales Log: A log of all trades processed on a stock along with the time and size of each trade.

Trading Floor: A floor where live trades are processed.

Trend Line: A stocks price points that when connected draw a line heading up, sideway or down.

Up tick and Downtick: A change in a quote that reflects a higher (up tick) or lower (downtick) price.

Whisper Number: An earnings number that circulates around the trading floor and brokerage houses that guesses at a stocks future earnings. A whisper number is not a firm number from an analyst, it is only an estimate.

Wiggle: A small quick price movement caused by market makers to shake out traders from their positions.